FOUNDATION MATERIAL FOR DOCTRINAL CATHOLIC ACTION

Based upon *"A Little Child's First Communion"*
For the Use of Teachers of Christian Doctrine in
Homes, Schools, Catechetical Centers, Training
Classes for Catechists, and Novitiates
Also for Leaders of Study Clubs

By MOTHER BOLTON
Religious of The Cenacle
*Author of "A Little Child's First Communion" and
"The Spiritual Way" Series of Textbooks*

WITH A FOREWORD BY HIS GRACE
THE MOST REVEREND
JOHN GREGORY MURRAY, S. T. D.
Archbishop of St. Paul

ST. AUGUSTINE ACADEMY PRESS
HOMER GLEN, ILLINOIS

Imprimi Potest.
FR. JEROME DAWSON, O. F. M.,
Minister Provincialis.

Nihil Obstat.
ARTHUR J. SCANLAN, S. T. D.,
Censor Librorum.

Imprimatur.
✠ PATRICK CARDINAL HAYES,
Archbishop of New York.

New York, July 25, 1938.

This book was originally published in 1938 by the Cenacle of St. Regis.

This facsimile edition, reprinted in 2021 by St. Augustine Academy Press,
is a direct reproduction of the 1941 edition by St. Anthony Guild Press.

ISBN: 978-1-64051-113-2

To

Very Reverend Mother Marie Majoux

Religious of The Cenacle

Who Greatly Desired

The Substantial Training of Teachers

of Religion

This Volume Is

Lovingly Dedicated

Foreword

In the field of catechetical activity much has been done in supplying texts for the use of the pupil, but very little has been done in a scientific development of aids to the teacher for a program of Christian Doctrine that is not limited to giving information but extends to the upbuilding of a Christian character that finds its highest achievement in the life of Catholic Action.

This lack of properly coördinated material, which may serve as a basis for the development of the teacher himself, has induced Mother Bolton to reveal to the world the rich treasures that she has acquired over a period of many years spent in the enrichment of her own religious character, and the instruction of others in the way of the spiritual life.

With great satisfaction have I gone over every sentence of her Foundation Material for Doctrinal Catholic Action, and I marvel at the abundance of priceless wisdom that she has gathered from the inspired word of the Scriptures, the riches of St. Augustine and St. Thomas and the wide experience that she has had in her personal career as a teacher.

Here indeed will the seeker after the best catechetical methods find an inexhaustible store that does credit to the author while it pays the high compliment to the student-teacher that the most profound learning of the Fathers is not too deep for the apostle of Christian Doctrine to assimilate or too obscure for her to impart to the soul that has been made docile to the mysteries of divine truth by the abundance of sacramental grace.

Not simply to know but to live the truth, not merely to desire but to possess the love, not only to receive but to give the fruits of a divine sacrifice should be the aim of every child of God incorporated in the Mystical Body of Christ. Only the living teacher imitating the Divine Teacher in the exemplification of virtue and power is qualified to impart such doctrine that leads to life and action. Mother Bolton has endeavored to show the way.

May those who make use of this volume find in it a challenge to rise to the heights of personal knowledge and apostolic power that are the necessary qualities in the souls of those whom Christ will gladly use to reveal His divine personality, extend His heavenly kingdom and glorify His Beloved Spouse, the Church of God!

✠ JOHN GREGORY MURRAY,
Archbishop of Saint Paul

Saint Paul, Minnesota
July 26, 1938.

Contents

BOOK ONE
God Is Love

BASAL MATERIAL

FOR

DISCUSSING OR TEACHING

BOOK ONE: GOD IS LOVE

Book One: God Is Love

A. INTRODUCTORY

The Code of Canon Law: Canon 854

That the TEACHER OF RELIGION may be sure of the mind of the Church concerning the requirements for First Holy Communion, Canon 854, Article 3, of the Code of Canon Law is here presented.

The Article reads:

"Outside the case of danger of death, a deeper knowledge of Christian Doctrine and a more accurate preparation is justly demanded, to an extent that they know at least the Mysteries of the Faith necessary as absolute means of salvation, and that they do approach Holy Communion with such devotion as can be expected from young children."

"A LITTLE CHILD'S FIRST COMMUNION" presents the fundamental doctrines of the Faith in simple form and language. It prepares the child for First Holy Communion according to "THE SPIRITUAL WAY" plan, and it is the beginning of "THE SPIRITUAL WAY" series.

If the spiritual foundation which should be laid in the First Communion preparation be inadequate and superficial, it will affect all of the subsequent religious teaching.

But it requires, on the part of the teacher, a broader background of theological and psychological knowledge to teach a little child in such a way as to lay a strong doctrinal foundation, than it does to teach doctrine in the upper grades.

"A LITTLE CHILD'S FIRST COMMUNION" is divided into six books covering the doctrine the child should be taught for First Communion. In presenting this doctrine to the child, PSYCHOLOGICAL LAWS ARE CAREFULLY HEEDED: that is, the doctrine is presented to the child in a normal, logical way which is in harmony with the child-mind, and therefore is both stimulating and satisfying.

1

Balancing Time
in Presenting the Fundamental Doctrines of the Faith

The time allowed for teaching each book could vary in accordance with the conditions under which the child is being prepared for First Communion. But the time should be so arranged that each section will receive its correct proportion of the time allotted for preparation.

Thus there is sufficient material for an enriched daily program in parochial schools, while in catechetical centers where time is abridged, all written work could be done outside of class.

The following table shows the correct balancing of subject-matter:

"A LITTLE CHILD'S FIRST COMMUNION"

Subjects Treated	Parochial Schools 180 Lessons	Catechetical Centers 40 Lessons	25 Lessons	20 Lessons
BOOK ONE:	22	5	3	3
God Is Love.				
Creation: God's Gifts of Love.				
BOOK TWO:	22	5	3	3
God Is Truth.				
Our First Parents.				
A Promise by the God of Truth.				
The Prophets.				
God's Own Son.				
BOOK THREE:	40	9	6	4
The Mother of God's Own Son.				
The Story of Saint Joseph.				
The Life of Jesus.				
The Blessed Trinity.				
The Commandments				

Subjects Treated	Parochial Schools 180 Lessons	Catechetical Centers		
		40 Lessons	25 Lessons	20 Lessons
BOOK FOUR:	46	10	6	4
Jesus' Church. The Holy Mass.				
BOOK FIVE:	27	6	4	3
The Sacraments: Baptism, Penance, Holy Eucharist. A Preparation for Confirmation.				
BOOK SIX:	23	5	3	3
The Sacraments: Extreme Unction, Holy Orders, Matrimony. A Preparation for First Holy Communion.				

The Child's Project Book

In preparing children for First Holy Communion, there should always be a close bond between the teacher and the father and mother of the child. Especially in catechetical centers, where it is at all possible, the interest of the parents should be sought after in helping the children at home to work out the tests given in "A Little Child's First Communion," and to draw or paste appropriate pictures in their Project Books. Under these pictures one, two or three correct sentences pertaining to the lesson should be written.

Each child should have his own Religion Project Book.

The interest of the parents should also be solicited in signing the review pages given throughout the series.

Central Dogmas

Throughout the world today, including our own country, the very fundamental doctrines of THE GODHEAD and THE DIVINITY OF CHRIST are being ignored or openly attacked. Our children are living in this atmosphere. Consequently one of our essential duties as teachers of religion is to emphasize and draw special attention to these central dogmas. SO IN OUR PREPARATION FOR FIRST HOLY COMMUNION, IS IT NOT LOGICAL AND BEST FOR THE CHILD'S SPIRITUAL FOUNDATION TO BEGIN WITH A STUDY OF THE GODHEAD?

And in planning a lesson on the Godhead, we must consider what ideas concerning God we would like to leave with the little child. But to decide this very important question in the way which will be best for the child, it is necessary to have both a good theological and a good psychological background.

The teaching of St. Thomas concerning the Godhead will surely be a right theological basis for planning a lesson even for the little child. The following quotations concerning the Godhead are taken from the teachings of St. Thomas:

"Because the Essence of God is His Intellect and Will, from the fact of His acting by His Essence it follows that He acts after the mode of Intellect and Will."

The function of the intellect is to know truth.

The Divine Intellect is always knowing All-Truth. And All-Truth is in God Himself.

"Not only is truth in Him, but HE ... IS TRUTH ... and FIRST TRUTH."

The function of the will is to love the good.

The Divine Will is always loving the All-Good. And God Himself is the All-Good.

"Love is the first movement of the will. . . . It has been shown that Will exists in God and hence we must attribute love to Him."

"GOD IS LOVE" (1 John 4:16).

In the Godhead, God the Father is First Principle. God the Father, knowing Himself, generates the Son, the Second Person of the Blessed Trinity.

As the Second Person of the Blessed Trinity proceeds from the Father by way of Intellect, He is called by various names pertaining to the intellect, such as THE WORD, THE WISDOM OF THE FATHER, THE TRUTH.

The Third Person of the Blessed Trinity, the Holy Ghost, proceeds from the Infinite Love between the Father and the Son, that is, by way of Will.

In the Blessed Trinity, the Holy Ghost is Love.

"There are two processions in God, one by way of the Intellect, which is the Word; and another by way of the Will, which is the procession of Love."

As TRUTH in the Godhead excites LOVE, logically, it would seem that the doctrinal statement, GOD IS TRUTH, should be taught first to the little child.

But experimentation shows that the little child's appreciation of love comes before his appreciation of truth. In the series, "A Little Child's First Communion," these doctrinal statements are presented in psychological order. So the teaching, GOD IS LOVE, precedes the teaching, GOD IS TRUTH.

A Book for Each Child

This First Communion series is written for the spiritual development of the child. So each child should have his own book. He should read the stories and reproduce them, and both silent and oral reading are suggested.

A STRONG, CONSTRUCTIVE, SPIRITUAL FOUNDATION WILL BE LAID IN THE SOUL OF THE CHILD THROUGH THE STUDY OF "A LITTLE CHILD'S FIRST COMMUNION"; AND BECAUSE OF THE APPLICATION OF PSYCHOLOGICAL PRINCIPLES, THIS TEACHING WILL BE A STIMULATION TO THE FURTHER STUDY OF DOCTRINE.

Sanctifying Grace

It is folly to try to teach a supernatural religion without, from the very beginning, putting the religious structure upon a supernatural foundation. Consequently any system of religious teaching that has not for its basis the doctrine of Sanctifying Grace must of necessity be futile.

The doctrinal principle, "God is the Creator," belongs to the natural order. It does not require as a background any teaching concerning Sanctifying Grace. The "soul" also belongs to the natural order. So teaching pertaining to the soul can also be given without a background of knowledge concerning the doctrine of Sanctifying Grace. But practically all our religious truths, with these and perhaps a few other exceptions, belong to the supernatural order and cannot be well taught and assimilated until teaching concerning the doctrine of Sanctifying Grace has been brought to the level of the child-mind.

In the series, "A Little Child's First Communion," the beginning teaching is that God is All-Love and All-Truth.

Further teaching makes known to the child that God is the Great Giver of Love and Truth.

And from the very beginning SANCTIFYING GRACE is taught as GOD'S LOVE AND TRUTH IN US, or GOD LIVING IN US.

In the presentation of the doctrine concerning Jesus' Church, in Book Four, the terms "God's Grace" and "the Light of Grace" are given; for at this stage of the doctrinal development, the child has had time to assimilate their meaning. And throughout Books Five and Six the terms "God's Grace" and "the Light of Grace" are used in connection with the teaching concerning the Sacraments.

In "The Spiritual Way" series which is a continuation of "A Little Child's First Communion" and contains religious teaching sufficient to cover a period of four years, the doctrine of Sanctifying Grace is taught in a way which corresponds with the more advanced teaching concerning God given in those books.

The Importance of Applying Psychological Principles
in Presenting Doctrinal Truths

To prepare food so that it can be assimilated by us demands TIME, ENERGY and SKILL on the part of more than one person. But it is never considered by us a waste of time, energy and skill to have food prepared for us three times a day. And we expect, as a matter of course, that it will be prepared in such a way that we can assimilate it.

All this expenditure is made willingly by us, in order to insure sufficient physical health and strength to live our lives, day by day, in a useful, happy and vigorous way.

To present Doctrinal Truths to a child in such a way that he can assimilate them demands also an expenditure of time, energy and skill on the part of the one presenting the Doctrinal Truths.

And does it not seem illogical and inconsistent on our part to be so willing to expend time, energy and skill to gain physical health and strength, and to be so very slow to recognize the absolute need of expending time, energy and skill in presenting Doctrinal Truths which, when assimilated, will lead to spiritual health and strength?

Are there recognized principles of education, or psychology, which will help us to present Doctrinal Truths to children so that they can assimilate them?

Yes, there are recognized principles.

And will the recognized educational and psychological principles of today be the same thirty or forty or fifty years hence?

True principles of education are based upon the nature and workings of the human mind. And the nature of the human mind will always remain the same — desirous of Truth and able to grasp it in a greater or lesser degree in accordance with the natural, logical and harmonious presentation of the Truth.

There are two processes by which the mind can arrive at Truth. And these two processes are exactly opposite in approach and effect.

By the DEDUCTIVE PROCESS the Doctrinal Truth is presented to the mind at the very beginning of the lesson. It is then explained and its applications are given.

By the INDUCTIVE PROCESS the mind is GRADUALLY led up to the Doctrinal Truth through a series of logical questions, always allowing time for the mind's reactions. In other words, by the inductive process the child himself is led to the Doctrinal Truth. This is the normal, natural way of learning.

It is the way in which the race has learned.

It is the way in which a child in its home usually learns.

It is the way to build up leaders. For if minds are moulded JUST TO ACCEPT TRUTHS without reaction, it may be an easy method of teaching, but it is a deadening process for the learner. It is mechanical instead of vital.

We have not generally made use of the inductive procedure in our teaching of Religion. And this is why we have not had the leaders so sorely needed.

This is why our Holy Father has urged Catholics to PREPARE THEM-SELVES for Catholic Action.

In the beginning of Christianity, the Christians were not given a book of theological statements to be memorized. They were taught Doctrine rationally by word of mouth. In this way they assimilated the Truths taught them. And we know that they possessed spiritual vigor and power.

At the present time if we require our children to memorize theological statements before the meaning of the statements has been slowly and logically developed, our children will not have spiritual power and they will not be leaders. But if, on the contrary, we teach each Doctrinal Truth so slowly and carefully that the child can assimilate it, even partially, that child will become a SPIRITUALLY FORCEFUL human being.

"A Little Child's First Communion," and all of "The Spiritual Way" series, teach Doctrine INDUCTIVELY and make use of the DEDUCTIVE process in presenting the applications of the principle.

Extract from the Decree "Quam Singularis"

"Both for the First Confession and First Communion a complete and perfect knowledge of Christian Doctrine is not necessary. The child will, however, be obliged GRADUALLY to learn the whole Catechism according to HIS ABILITY."

The series of six books, "A Little Child's First Communion," fulfills fully the requirements of Canon 854, and this series can be completed in the SECOND GRADE.

"The Spiritual Way" is a gradual development of all the doctrinal statements given in the Catechism. This gradual development is adapted to the mental age of the child, thus fulfilling the requirements of the decree "Quam Singularis" issued by Pope Pius X, August 8, 1910.

An Apostolic Benediction

From a letter written by E. Cardinal Pacelli, the Secretary of State to His Holiness Pope Pius XI, dated February 21, 1930, we have the assurance that His Holiness gives his approval to "The Spiritual Way" system of presenting Doctrine.

"HAPPY TO SEE THE GOOD RESULTS OF THIS METHOD OF TEACHING THE CATECHISM IN THE SCHOOLS OF THE UNITED STATES AND REJOICING IN THE BELIEF THAT THESE RESULTS WILL BE MULTIPLIED ELSEWHERE, HIS HOLINESS WITH ALL HIS HEART GIVES, AS A MARK OF HIS PATERNAL AFFECTION AND AS A GUARANTEE OF THE BEST OF HEAVENLY BLESSINGS UPON THIS WORK, HIS SPECIAL APOSTOLIC BENEDICTION."

B. DOCTRINAL TRUTHS PRESENTED TO THE CHILD IN BOOK ONE WITH THE EXPECTATION THAT HE WILL UNDERSTAND AND APPRECIATE THEM IN ACCORDANCE WITH HIS MENTAL AGE:

That:

1. there is a Superior Personal Invisible Divine Being — a First Cause — and — that all things created come from Him as expressions of Divine Love;

2. God is All-Good and All-Lovable;

3. God is Love;

4. God loves us;

5. the concrete material gift among friends is but the token of something more real, though abstract: Love. "For since the creation of the world His invisible attributes, His everlasting power and divinity — are to be discerned and contemplated in His works" (Romans 1:20);

6. God gives us of His Love as well as His other gifts;

7. we are children of God when we participate in His Love (Sanctifying Grace);

8. we become more like God as we have more of His Love in us;

9. we should worship God by Faith, Hope and Love.

C. GROWTH IN POWER TO BE EXPECTED IN THE CHILD AS A RESULT OF STUDYING BOOK ONE:

Greater facility:

1. in interpreting the printed page;

2. in giving oral expression to the interpreted thought;

3. in grasping the more difficult lessons of Book Two;

4. in knowing God as All-Love;

5. in loving God through meditations on His Goodness to us;

6. in praying to God as a child to his father;

7. in making a Catechism Project Book.

D. PEDAGOGICAL STRUCTURE

In the teaching of secular subjects, it is generally conceded that pedagogical procedures are important. We think that they are of equal importance in the teaching of religion.

The following is an outline of the pedagogical procedures used in teaching the unit of doctrine, "God Is Love."

Teacher's Major Objective

To develop in the child-mind correct ideas concerning the Personality and Nature of God and our relationship with Him through Sanctifying Grace.

Exploration and Establishment of an Apperceptive Background for the New Knowledge

This part of the lesson is an exploration into the child's mind, to discover what he already knows which would dovetail into the new subject-matter about to be presented and establish an appropriate apperceptive background for it.

Motivation

Stories, statements, questions or problems which would create in the child-mind a desire for the new knowledge to be given in the PRESENTATION of the lesson.

Presentation of New Knowledge

Generalizations

Applications and Related Activities

h. Project work

1. To illustrate the text, children may make original drawings, or cut
    from magazines appropriate pictures. Under each picture one or
    more explanatory sentences should be written. (Use no pictures rep-
    resenting God, and do not use a picture of our Lord in illustrating
    the text of Book One.)

2. Suggested Pictures for Book One

    a. Tom and his dog; Ann and her clock.
    b. Animals or scenes with animals.
    c. Scenes with trees, flowers, grass.
    d. Sun, moon and stars.
    e. Oceans, lakes, rivers, glaciers.
    f. Family groups, fathers, mothers, brothers and sisters.
    g. A child looking up at the sky.
    h. God's Gifts of Love: trees, flowers, birds, etc.
    i. Children on their way to church or school.
    j. Children talking to their mother; children talking to a priest.
    k. Decorative schemes for Acts and Tests.

E. THEOLOGICAL BACKGROUND *

A good teacher of religion in any grade, even the lowest, should teach from a rich theological background, and to do this the teacher must know the mind of the Church, as explained by her great Doctors.

The following excerpts from St. Augustine and St. Thomas Aquinas will illumine the seemingly very simple doctrinal statements presented in the book, "God Is Love."

1. Power in the Godhead

a. "For this name of God by which He is called could not but be known to every creature, even to all nations, before they believed on Christ. For such is the power of true Godhead that it cannot be altogether and utterly hidden from the rational creature, once it makes use of its reason. For, with the exception of a few in whom nature is excessively depraved, the whole human race confesses God to be the author of the world."

St. Augustine, "In Joan. Evang.," CVI, 4.

b. "Power is not predicated of God as something really differing from His Knowledge and Will, but differing only in our notion of them."

St. Thomas Aquinas, "Summa Theologica,"
Part One, First Number, Q. XXV, Art. I.

2. In God There Exist Intellect and Will

a. "There exists WILL in God; as there is INTELLECT . . . and as His Intellect is His own Existence, so is His Will."

Ibid., Q. XIX, Art. I.

b. "Because the ESSENCE OF GOD IS HIS INTELLECT AND WILL, from the fact of His acting by His Essence, it follows that He acts after the mode of Intellect and Will."

Ibid., Art. IV.

* Acknowledgment, with appreciation, is given to Sheed & Ward, New York, for permission to quote passages from *An Augustine Synthesis*, arranged by Erich Przywara, S. J.

3. The Processions in God

a. "There are two processions in God, one by way of the Intellect, which is the procession of the Word; and another by way of the Will which is the procession of Love."

    Ibid., Second Number, Q. XXXVII, Art. I.

b. "These processions are two only, . . . one derived from the action of the Intellect, the procession of the Word; and the other from the action of the Will, the procession of Love."

    Ibid., Q. XXVIII, Art. IV.

4. God Is Love

a. "God is the same as His Essence or Nature."

    Ibid., First Number, Q. III, Art. III.

b. "It has been shown that WILL exists in God and hence we must attribute LOVE to Him."

    Ibid., Q. XX, Art. I.

c. "John says: 'God is Love' (1 John 4:16). Love must necessarily be in God. Love is the first movement of the will and of every appetitive faculty."

    Ibid.

5. We Cannot See God

a. "It is impossible for God to be seen by the sense of sight or by any other sense or faculty of the sensitive power. . . . Hence He cannot be seen by the sense or the imagination, but only by the intellect."

    Ibid., Q. XII, Art. III.

b. "For since as yet 'we walk by faith and not by sight' (2 Corinthians 5:7), we certainly do not yet see God . . . 'face to face' (1 Corinthians 13:12); Whom, however, we shall never see, unless we already love Him now. But who loves what he does not know?

    "It is of course possible for something to be known and not loved; but I ask whether it be possible for what is not known to be loved; since if it cannot, then no one loves God before he knows Him.

    "And what is it to know God except to conceive Him and steadfastly perceive Him with the mind? For He is not a body to be searched out by the eyes of the flesh.

"Again, before we have the power to conceive and perceive God, as He can be conceived and perceived — for this is permitted to the clean of heart, since 'Blessed are the clean of heart: for they shall see God' (Matthew 5:8) — unless He be loved by faith, it will not be possible for the heart to be cleansed so that it may be apt and meet to see Him."

St. Augustine, "De. Trin.," VIII, IV, 6; IX, 13.

6. God Gives Us of His Love

a. "In order that we might receive that love whereby we should love, we were ourselves loved, while as yet we had it not. . . . For we would not have wherewithal to love Him, unless we received it from Him by His first loving us."

St. Augustine, "De Grat. Christ," XXVI, 27.

b. "In the justification of the impious justice is seen, when God remits sins for the sake of LOVE, though He Himself has mercifully infused that LOVE."

St. Thomas Aquinas, loc. cit., Q. XXI, Art. IV.

c. "Whatever is pleasing to God in a man is caused by the Divine Love."

Ibid., Part Two, Third Number, Q. CX, Art. I.

d. "For God is in all things by His essence, power and presence, according to His one common mode, as the cause existing in the effects which participate in His goodness.

"Above and beyond this common mode, however, there is one special mode belonging to the rational nature wherein God is said to be present as the object known is in the knower, and the beloved in the lover. And since the rational creature by its own operation of knowledge and love attains to God Himself, according to this special mode, God is said not only to exist in the rational creature, but also to dwell therein as in His own temple. So no other effect can be put down as the reason why the Divine Person is in the rational creature in a new mode, except SANCTIFYING GRACE."

Ibid., Part One, Second Number, Q. XLIII, Art. III.

e. "And thus because the soul participates in the Divine Goodness imperfectly, THE PARTICIPATION OF THE DIVINE GOODNESS, WHICH IS GRACE, has its being in the soul in a less perfect way than the soul subsists in itself."

Ibid., Part Two (First Part), Third Number, Q. CX, Art. II.

f. "The gift of grace surpasses every capability of created nature, since it is nothing short of A PARTAKING OF THE DIVINE NATURE which exceeds every other nature."

                                             Ibid., Q. CXII, Art. I.

g. "And this is what Augustine says ('De Natura et Gratia,' XXXI): 'It [grace] is prevenient, inasmuch as it heals, and subsequent, inasmuch as, being healed, we are strengthened; it is prevenient, inasmuch as we are called, and subsequent, inasmuch as we are glorified.' GOD'S LOVE signifies something eternal; and hence can never be called anything but prevenient."

                                           Ibid., Q. CXI, Art. III.

h. "Now the effect of the DIVINE LOVE in us, which is taken away by sin, is GRACE, whereby a man is made worthy of eternal life, from which sin shuts him out. Hence we could not conceive the remission of guilt without the infusion of grace."

                                           Ibid., Q. CXIII, Art. II.

i. "Sanctifying grace disposes the soul to possess the Divine Person; and this is signified when it is said that the Holy Ghost is given according to the gift of grace. Nevertheless the gift itself of grace is from the Holy Ghost; which is meant by the words, THE CHARITY OF GOD IS POURED FORTH IN OUR HEARTS BY THE HOLY GHOST."

                   Ibid., Part One, Second Number, Q. XLIII, Art. III.

j. "Moreover the Holy Ghost is possessed by man, and dwells within him in the very gift itself of SANCTIFYING GRACE."

                                                 Ibid.

k. "The soul is made like to God by grace. Hence for a Divine Person to be sent to anyone by grace, there must needs be a likening of the soul to the Divine Person Who is sent, by some gift of grace. Because the Holy Ghost is Love, THE SOUL IS ASSIMILATED TO THE HOLY GHOST BY THE GIFT OF CHARITY; hence the mission of the Holy Ghost is according to the mode of charity. Whereas the Son is the Word, not any sort of word, but One Who breathes forth Love."

                                           Ibid., Art. V.

7. We Should Ask God to Give Us More and More of His Love

a. "Whoever has grace, by this very fact becomes fitted for eternal life."

                                   Ibid., First Number, Q. XXIV, Art. III.

b. "The good of grace in one is greater than the good of nature in the whole universe."

            Ibid., Part Two (First Part), Third Number, Q. CXIII, Art. 9.

8.   God Is Our Father: He Wants Us to Love Him

a.   "Now it is manifest from the foregoing (QQ. XXVII and XXVIII) that the perfect idea of Paternity and Filiation is to be found in God the Father, and in God the Son, because one is the Nature and Glory of the Father and the Son. But in the creature, filiation is found in relation to God; not in a perfect manner, since the Creator and the creature have not the same nature, but by way of a certain likeness, which is the more perfect the nearer we approach to the true idea of filiation. For God is called the Father of some creatures by reason only of a trace (*vestigium*) as that which is found in irrational creatures, according to the words, 'Who is the Father of the rain? Or Who begot the drops of dew?' (Job 38:28). Of the rational creature [He is the Father] by reason of the likeness of His image, according to the text, 'Is He not thy Father, Who possessed, and made, and created thee?' (Deuteronomy 32:6).

"And of others, HE IS THE FATHER BY SIMILITUDE OF GRACE, and these are also called adoptive sons, as ordained to the heritage of eternal glory by the gift of grace which they have received, according to the text, 'THE SPIRIT HIMSELF GIVES TESTIMONY to our spirit that we are the sons of God; and if sons heirs also' (Romans 8:16, 17)."

Ibid., Part One, Second Number, Q. XXXIII, Art. III.

b.   "He alone has a proper love of himself who loves God. . . . Thou lovest thyself wholesomely if thou lovest God more than thyself. That, therefore, which thou aimest at in thyself, thou must aim at in thy neighbor, namely, that he may love God with a love which is perfect."

St. Augustine, "De. Mor. Eccl.," I, XXVI, 48, 49

c.   "When I set before the eyes of my heart, such as they be, the intellectual beauty of Him out of Whose mouth nothing false proceedeth, though my weak and throbbing senses are driven back where truth in her radiance doth more and more brighten upon me, yet I am so inflamed with love of that surpassing comeliness, that I despise all human considerations which would recall me thence."

St. Augustine, "Contra mend.," XVIII, 36.

d.   "Now it is manifest that the good of the part is for the good of the whole; hence everything, by its natural appetite and love, loves its own proper good on account of the common good of the whole universe, which is God. Hence Dionysius says that GOD LEADS EVERYTHING TO LOVE OF HIMSELF.

"Hence in the state of perfect nature man referred the love of himself and of all other things to the love of God as to its end; and thus he loved God more than himself and above all things.

"But in the state of corrupt nature man falls short of this in the appetite of his rational will, which, unless it is cured by God's grace, follows its private good on account of the corruption of nature.

"And hence we must say that in the state of perfect nature man did not need the gift of grace added to his natural endowments, in order to love God above all things naturally, although he needed God's help to move him to it; but in the state of corrupt nature man needs, even for this, the help of grace to heal his nature."

St. Thomas Aquinas, op. cit.,
Part Two (First Part), Third Number, Q. CIX, Art. III.

9.   The Lord Keepeth All Them That Love Him

a. "It is necessary to attribute PROVIDENCE to God.

"We must say, however, that all things are subject to Divine Providence not only in general, but even in their individual selves.

"Since a rational creature has, through the possession of free will, control over its actions, it is subject to Divine Providence in an especial manner."

Ibid., Part One,
First Number, Q. XXII, Art. I and II.

10.   God Is the Supreme Good

a. " 'The Lord is good' (Psalm 134:3). But good not in the same manner as the things which He hath made are good. For God made all things not merely good, but very good (Genesis 1:31).

"He made the heaven and the earth and all things which are in them good, and He made them very good.

"If he made all these things good, of what kind is He Who made them? And yet since He made them good, and He Who made is much better than the things which He made, you can find nothing better to speak of Him than that 'the Lord is good,' if at any rate you understand Him to be good in a peculiar sense, from whom all other good things proceed. For He made all things good, He Himself is good, Whom no one made.

"He is good by His own goodness, not by any good derived from elsewhere. HE BY HIS OWN GOOD, THAT IS HIMSELF, IS GOOD, NOT BY ADHERING TO SOME OTHER GOOD."

St. Augustine, "In Ps. CXXXIV," 3.

b. "How good must that be from which all good things proceed? You can find no good at all which is not good from Him, as He is properly THE GOOD which makes all things good."

Ibid., 4.

c. "God is the Supreme Good. . . . Good is attributed to God, as was said in the preceding article, inasmuch as all desirable perfections flow from Him as from their first cause."

St. Thomas Aquinas, op. cit., Part I, First Number, Q. VI, Art. II.

d. "God alone is good by His own Essence. . . . The goodness of a creature is not its essence but something superadded."

Ibid., Art. III.

e. "It belongs to the essence of goodness to communicate itself to others."

Ibid., Part Three, First Number, Q. I, Art. I.

11. All Created Things Are God's Gifts of Love

a. "Ask the loveliness of the earth, ask the loveliness of the sea, ask the loveliness of the wide airy spaces, ask the loveliness of the sky, ask the order of the stars, ask the sun making the day light with its beams, ask the moon tempering the darkness of the night that follows, ask the living things which move in the waters, which tarry on the land, which fly in the air; ask the souls that are hidden, the bodies that are perceptive; the visible things which must be governed, the invisible things which govern — ask all these things, and they will all answer thee, Lo, see we are lovely. Their loveliness is their confession. And these lovely but mutable things, who has made them, save Beauty immutable?"

St. Augustine, "Serm. CCXLI," II, 2; 111, 3.

b. "All these beautiful things which you see, which you love, He made. If these are beautiful, what is He Himself? If these are great, how great must He be? Therefore from those things which we love here, let us the more long for Him: that by that very love we may purify our hearts by faith, and His vision, when it comes, may find our hearts purified."

St. Augustine, "In Ps. LXXXIV," 9.

c. "God from Whom flow to us all good things, by Whom all evil things are kept from us.

"God, above Whom is nothing, beyond Whom is nothing, without Whom is nothing.

"God, under Whom all is, in Whom all is, with Whom all is."

St. Augustine, "Solil. I," i, 4.

d. "For He produced things into being in order that His goodness might be communicated to creatures and be represented by them; and because His goodness could not be adequately represented by one creature alone, He produced many and diverse creatures, that what was wanting to one in the representation of the Divine Goodness might be supplied by another."

> St. Thomas Aquinas, op. cit., Part One,
> Second Number, Q. XLVII, Art. I.

e. "Everything which is not the Divine Essence is a creature."

> Ibid., Q. XXVIII, Art. II.

f. "The nature of man requires that he be led to the invisible by visible things. So the invisible things of God must be made manifest to man by the things that are visible."

> Ibid., Q. XLIII, Art. VII.

12.   "To Save Our Souls We Must Worship God by Faith, Hope and Charity" (Catechism)

a. "Now the theological virtues, FAITH, HOPE and CHARITY, have an act in reference to God as their proper object: . . . and so Augustine says that God is worshiped by faith, hope and charity."

> Ibid., Part Two
> (Second Part), Q. LXXXI, Art. V.

b. "Understanding is the reward of faith. Therefore seek not to understand that thou mayest believe, but believe that thou mayest understand."

> St. Augustine, "In Joan. Evang.," XXIX, 6.

c. "A right faith is the beginning of a good life, and to this also eternal life is due. Now it is faith to believe that which you do not yet see; and the reward of this faith is to see that which you believe. In the time of faith, therefore, as in a seeding time, let us not weaken. To the very end let us not weaken, but let us persevere until we gather that which we have sown."

> St. Augustine, "Serm.," XLIII, i, 1.

d. "We shall see Him face to face, if we now see Him by faith. Let our faith have eyes, and its truth shall be displayed. Let us believe in Him Whom we see not, and rejoicing we shall see, and we shall enjoy Him seen."

> St. Augustine, "In Ps. XCVII," 3.

e. "Love, and do what thou wilt; whether thou hold thy peace, of love hold thy peace; whether thou cry out, of love cry out; whether thou correct, of love correct; whether thou spare, through love do thou spare; let the root of love be within, of this root can nothing spring but what is good."

> St. Augustine, "In Epist. Joannis ad Parthos," Tr. VII, 8.

13. God Hears Our Prayers

a. "Augustine says in the Prospers 'Liber Sententiarum' (Sent. CCXII): 'He who faithfully prays God for the necessaries of this life, is both mercifully heard and mercifully not heard. For the physician knows better than the sick man what is good for the disease.' "

> St. Thomas Aquinas, loc. cit., Q. LXXXIII, Art. XV.

b. "As to its efficacy in impetrating, prayer derives this from the grace of God to Whom we pray, and Who instigates us to pray. Wherefore Augustine says ('De Verb. Dom., Serm. V,' XXIX): 'He would not urge us to ask unless He were willing to give'; and Chrysostom on Luke XVIII says: 'He never refuses to grant our prayers, since in His loving kindness He urged us not to faint in praying.' "

> Ibid., Q. LXXXIII, Art. XV.

F. BIBLICAL BACKGROUND

Do you not think that a good TEACHER OF RELIGION in any grade should desire to have a fair knowledge of the Bible texts from both the Old and the New Testaments concerning the points of doctrine presented in the books being used by the children?

Teachers having such a desire will find that a study of the following Bible texts, in addition to the theological excerpts just studied, will further illumine for them the doctrinal statements in the book, "God Is Love."

1. God's Gifts of Love

a. Genesis 1:1-31

"In the beginning God created HEAVEN and EARTH.

"And the earth was void and empty, and darkness was upon the face of the deep: and the Spirit of God moved over the waters.

"And God said: Be LIGHT made. And light was made.

"And God saw the LIGHT that IT WAS GOOD; . . .

"And God said: Let there be A FIRMAMENT. . . .

"God also said: Let the WATERS that are under the heaven, be gathered together into one place: and let the DRY LAND appear. And it was so done.

"And God called the dry land, EARTH: And the gathering together of the waters, He called SEAS. And God saw that IT WAS GOOD.

"And He said: Let the earth bring forth the GREEN HERB, and such as may seed and the FRUIT TREE yielding fruit after its kind, which may have seed in itself upon the earth. . . .

"And God said: Let there be LIGHTS made in the firmament of heaven. . . .

"And God made two GREAT LIGHTS: A GREATER LIGHT to rule the day; and a LESSER LIGHT to rule the night; and the STARS.

"And He set them in the firmament of heaven to shine upon the earth. . . .

"And God said: Let the waters bring forth the CREEPING CREATURE having life, and the FOWL that may fly over the earth. . . . And

God created the GREAT WHALES, and EVERY LIVING and MOVING CREATURE, which the waters brought forth, according to their kinds, and every WINGED FOWL according to its kind. And God saw that IT WAS GOOD. . . .

"And God said: Let the earth bring forth the LIVING CREATURE in its kind, CATTLE AND CREEPING THINGS, and BEASTS OF THE EARTH, according to their kinds. And it was so done. . . . And God saw that IT WAS GOOD.

"And He said: Let us make MAN to our image and likeness: and let him have dominion over the fishes of the sea, and the fowls of the air, and the beasts, and the whole earth, and every creeping creature. . . .

"And GOD CREATED MAN TO HIS OWN IMAGE: to the image of God He created him: MALE and FEMALE He created them. . . .

"And God said: Behold I HAVE GIVEN YOU every herb bearing seed . . . and all the trees . . . and . . . all beasts of the earth. . . .

"And God saw all the things that He had made, and THEY WERE VERY GOOD. . . . "

b. Job 38

The Power and Wisdom of God.

c. Psalm 4:7

". . . Thou hast given GLADNESS in my heart."

Psalm 8:4

"For I will behold Thy heavens, the works of Thy fingers: THE MOON AND THE STARS which Thou hast founded."

Psalm 8:6

"Thou hast made him [man] A LITTLE LESS THAN THE ANGELS, Thou hast crowned him with glory and honor."

Psalm 32:6, 7

"By the word of the Lord the HEAVENS were established: and all the power of them by the spirit of His mouth. Gathering together the WATERS OF THE SEA, as in a vessel. . . . "

Psalm 32:9

"For He spoke and they were made: He commanded and they were created."

Psalm 49:10, 11

"For all the BEASTS of the woods are Mine: the CATTLE on the hills, and the OXEN. I know all the FOWLS of the air: and with Me is the BEAUTY of the field."

Psalm 103:1-28

Thanking God for Gifts of Love.

d. Daniel 3:24-90

The Prayer and Canticle of Praise of the three holy children in the fiery furnace.

e. John 1:3

"ALL THINGS were made by Him: and without Him was made nothing that was made."

f. Acts 14:14

" ... the living God, Who made the HEAVEN, and the EARTH, and the SEA, and ALL THINGS that are in them."

Acts 14:16

" ... DOING GOOD from heaven, giving RAINS and FRUIT-FUL SEASONS, FILLING OUR HEARTS with food and gladness."

g. I Corinthians 4:7

" ... Or what hast thou that thou hast not received? ... "

2. We Cannot See the One Who Gave Us
These Gifts of Love

a. John 1:18; I John 4:12

"No man hath seen God at any time. . . . "

b. John 4:24

"God is a spirit. . . . "

c. I Timothy 6:16

" . . . Whom no man hath seen, nor can see. . . . "

3. God Is All-Good

a. Matthew 19:17

" . . . One is GOOD, God . . . " (Douay).
" . . . One alone there is who is GOOD . . . " (Westminster).

b. Mark 10:18

" . . . None is GOOD but one, THAT IS GOD."

c. Luke 18:19

" . . . None is GOOD but GOD ALONE."

4. God Is Love

a. John 3:16

"For God so loved the world, as TO GIVE HIS ONLY BE-GOTTEN SON. . . . "

b. 2 Corinthians 13:11

" . . . And THE GOD OF PEACE AND OF LOVE SHALL BE WITH YOU."

c. I John 4:8

"He that loveth not, knoweth not God: for GOD IS CHARITY" (Douay).
"For GOD IS LOVE" (Westminster).

I John 4:16

"And we have known, and have believed the charity which God hath to us. GOD IS CHARITY: and he that abideth in charity, abideth in God, and God in him" (Douay).

"And we have come to know and have believed the love which God hath in us. GOD IS LOVE. And whoso abideth in love, abideth in God and God abideth in him" (Westminster).

5.   God Gives Us of His Love

a. Jeremias 31:3

"... Yea, I have loved thee with an everlasting love, therefore have I drawn thee, taking pity on thee."

b. John 14:23

"... and We will come to him and make Our abode with him."

c. Romans 5:5

"... the charity of God is poured forth in our hearts by the Holy Ghost, Who is given to us."

Romans 8:39

"Nor height, nor depth, nor any other creature, shall be able to separate us from the love of God. ... "

d. 2 Thessalonians 2:15

"... God, and our Father, Who hath loved us, and hath given us everlasting consolation, and good hope in grace."

6.   When God's Love Is in Us We Are His Dear Children

a. Romans 8:14

"For whosoever are led by the Spirit of God, they are the SONS OF GOD."

Romans 8:15

"... But you have received the spirit of ADOPTION OF SONS, whereby we cry: Abba (Father)."

b. Ephesians 4:6

"One God and Father of all, Who is above all, and through all, AND IN US ALL."

c. 1 John 3:1, 2

"Behold what manner of charity the Father hath bestowed upon us, that we should be called, and should be the SONS OF GOD. ... "

7. God Is Our Father

a. I Paralipomenon 29:10

"... Blessed art Thou, O Lord the God of Israel, our FATHER."

b. Isaias 63:16

"... Thou, O Lord, art our FATHER, our Redeemer, from everlasting is Thy name."

c. Matthew 5:45

"That you may be the children of your FATHER Who is in heaven...."

Matthew 5:48

"Be you therefore perfect, as also your heavenly FATHER is perfect."

Matthew 6:1

"... otherwise you shall not have a reward of your FATHER."

Matthew 6:6

"... pray to thy FATHER in secret: and thy FATHER Who seeth in secret will repay thee."

Matthew 6:9

"Thus therefore shall you pray: Our FATHER Who art in heaven... "

Matthew 6:14

"... your heavenly FATHER will forgive you also your offences."

d. Luke 11:2

"... When you pray say: FATHER, hallowed be Thy name...."

Luke 12:30

"... your FATHER knoweth that you have need of these things."

e. Philippians 4:20

"Now to God and our FATHER be glory world without end."

8. Faith

a. Romans 5:1
"Being justified therefore by FAITH...."

Romans 5:2
"By whom also we have access through FAITH...."

b. I Corinthians 16:13
"Watch ye, stand fast in the FAITH, do manfully and be strengthened."

c. 2 Corinthians 5:7
"For we walk by FAITH, and not by sight."

d. Galatians 5:5
"For we in spirit, by FAITH, wait for the hope of justice."

Galatians 5:6
"...neither circumcision availeth anything, nor uncircumcision: but FAITH that worketh by charity."

e. I Timothy 6:12
"Fight the good fight of FAITH...."

f. Hebrews 11:1
"Now FAITH is the substance of things to be hoped for, the evidence of things that appear not."

Hebrews 11:3
"By FAITH we understand that the world was framed by the word of God...."

Hebrews 11:6
"But without FAITH it is impossible to please God. For he that cometh to God must believe that He is, and is a rewarder to them that seek Him."

g. I John 5:4
"...this is the victory which overcometh the world, our FAITH."

9. Hope

a. Psalm 4:10

"For Thou, O Lord, singularly hast settled me in HOPE."

Psalm 15:9

". . . moreover my flesh also shall rest in HOPE."

Psalm 30:25

"Do ye manfully, and let your heart be strengthened, all ye that HOPE in the Lord."

Psalm 32:18

"Behold the eyes of the Lord are on them that fear Him: and on them that HOPE in His mercy."

Psalm 32:22

"Let Thy mercy, O Lord, be upon us, as we have HOPED in Thee."

Psalm 38:8

"And now what is my HOPE? Is it not the Lord?"

Psalm 41:6, 7

"Why art thou sad, O my soul? . . . HOPE in God. . . . "

Psalm 70:5

"For Thou art my patience, O Lord; my HOPE, O Lord from my youth."

b. Proverbs 14:32

". . . but the just hath HOPE in His death."

c. Ecclesiasticus 2:11

". . . know ye that no one hath HOPED in the Lord, and hath been confounded."

d. Jeremias 17:13

"O Lord, THE HOPE OF ISRAEL: all that forsake Thee shall be confounded. . . ."

Jeremias 17:17

"... Thou art my HOPE in the day of affliction."

e. Lamentations 3:25

"The Lord is good to them that HOPE in Him, to the soul that seeketh Him."

f. Romans 5:2

"... glory in the HOPE of the glory of the sons of God."

Romans 5:3, 4

"... but we glory also in tribulations, knowing that tribulation worketh patience; and patience trial; and trial HOPE."

Romans 5:5

"And HOPE confoundeth not. . . ."

Romans 8:24

"For we are saved by HOPE."

Romans 8:25

"But if we HOPE for that which we see not, we wait for it with patience."

Romans 15:4

"... that through patience and the comfort of the Scriptures, we might have HOPE."

Romans 15:13

"Now the God of HOPE fill you with all joy ... that you may abound in HOPE. . . ."

g. Hebrews 10:23

"Let us hold fast the confession of our HOPE without wavering. . . ."

h. I Peter 1:3

"Blessed be the God and Father of our Lord Jesus Christ ... Who hath regenerated us unto a lively HOPE. . . ."

10. Charity (Love of God)

a. Deuteronomy 6:5

"Thou shalt LOVE the Lord thy God with thy whole heart and with thy whole soul, and with thy whole strength."

Deuteronomy 11:1

"Therefore LOVE the Lord thy God and observe His precepts and ceremonies. . . ."

b. Psalm 30:24

"O LOVE the Lord, all ye His saints: for the Lord will require truth. . . . "

Psalm 96:10

"You that LOVE the Lord, hate evil. . . ."

Psalm 144:20

"The Lord keepeth all them that LOVE Him. . . . "

c. Proverbs 10:12

" . . . CHARITY covereth all sins."

d. Canticles 8:7

"Many waters cannot quench CHARITY, neither can the floods drown it: if a man should give all the substance of his house for LOVE, he shall despise it as nothing."

e. Ecclesiasticus 1:14

"The LOVE of God is honorable wisdom."

Ecclesiasticus 7:32

"With all thy strength LOVE Him that made thee; and forsake not His ministers."

Ecclesiasticus 13:18

"LOVE God all thy life, and call upon Him for thy salvation."

f. Matthew 22:37

"Jesus said to him: Thou shalt LOVE the Lord thy God, with thy whole heart, and with thy whole soul, and with thy whole mind."

g. Mark 12:30

"And thou shalt LOVE the Lord thy God with thy whole heart, and with thy whole soul and with thy whole mind, and with thy whole strength. . . ."

h. Luke 10:27

" . . . Thou shalt LOVE the Lord thy God with thy whole heart, and with thy whole soul, and with all thy strength, and with all thy mind. . . . "

i. Romans 8:28

"And we know that to them that LOVE God, all things work together unto good. . . ."

j. I Corinthians 8:3

"But if any man LOVE God, the same is known by Him."

I Corinthians 13

Entire chapter.

I Corinthians 14:1

"Follow after CHARITY. . . ."

k. Ephesians 1:4

"As He chose us in Him before the foundation of the world, that we should be holy and unspotted in His sight in CHARITY."

l. I Peter 4:8

" . . . CHARITY covereth a multitude of sins."

m. I John 4:19

"Let us therefore LOVE God, because God first hath LOVED us."

n. 2 John 1:6

"And this is CHARITY, that we walk according to His commandments. . . ."

11. Faith — Hope — Charity

a. Ecclesiasticus 2:8-10

"Ye that fear the Lord, BELIEVE Him: and your reward shall not be made void. Ye that fear the Lord, HOPE in Him. Ye that fear the Lord LOVE Him, and your hearts shall be enlightened."

Ecclesiasticus 2:18

"They that fear the Lord WILL NOT BE INCREDULOUS to His word: and they that LOVE Him will keep His way."

Ecclesiasticus 34:15

"For their HOPE is on Him that saveth them, and the eyes of God are upon them that LOVE Him."

b. I Corinthians 13:13

"And now there remain FAITH, HOPE and CHARITY, these three: but the greatest of these is CHARITY."

c. Galatians 5:5, 6

"For we in spirit, by FAITH, wait for the HOPE of justice.... but FAITH that worketh by CHARITY."

d. I Timothy 1:5

"Now the end of the commandment is CHARITY, from a pure heart and a good conscience, and an unfeigned FAITH."

I Timothy 6:11

"But thou, O man of God, fly these things: and pursue justice, godliness, FAITH, CHARITY, patience, mildness."

e. 2 Timothy 2:22

"... pursue justice, FAITH, CHARITY and peace...."

f. Hebrews 10:22-24

"Let us draw near with a true heart in fulness of FAITH, ... Let us hold fast the confession of our HOPE without wavering, ... and let us consider one another, to provoke unto CHARITY...."

BOOK TWO
God Is Truth

BASAL MATERIAL

FOR

DISCUSSING OR TEACHING

BOOK TWO: GOD IS TRUTH

37

Book Two: God Is Truth

A. INTRODUCTORY

Spiritual Growth Necessitates Mind and Will Activity

The Catholic Church teaches us, her children, that when we are sharing in God's Love and Truth, that is, in the Divine Life, our acts have a special importance in God's sight, provided these acts have been given due consideration by our minds and their performance directed by our wills.

So any act against God's law — for instance, a violation of truth — which is a sin if the mind understands and the will directs it, is no sin if the mind does not understand and the will does not direct it.

And just as, under normal conditions, there can be no sin when the mind and the will are not acting, neither can there be any spiritual growth. For although everyone who is sharing in God's Love and Truth is in a state of holiness, no one can GROW spiritually unless his mind THINKS in accordance with THE MIND OF THE CHURCH, the authentic Teacher of Christ's principles, and his will ACTS in accordance with these principles.

Consequently, adequate Catholic training never consists in the mere presentation of knowledge. Although faithful teachers of Christian Doctrine seek after a correct and scientific presentation of doctrinal Truth, they are sure to value THE GOOD MIND AND WILL TRAINING accompanying this presentation more than the knowledge presented. For they never forget the biggest point of all, namely, that God wants His Own Image and Likeness made clear and bright in the soul of every child, through the possession of Sanctifying Grace and the right use of his mind and will.

Thus they know that the most vital work entrusted to their care is the developing and strengthening of God's Image and Likeness in the souls of the children to whom they are privileged to teach Christ's principles, that is, Christian Doctrine.

39

Book One taught the child the vital doctrinal truth, GOD IS LOVE. In presenting this truth, right psychological principles were followed. THE AIM was to make this important and fundamental concept, GOD IS LOVE, a vital factor in the child's life.

Now, in order to create in the child's mind balanced ideas concerning God, the second concept, GOD IS TRUTH, is presented in Book Two. And this latter theological statement is more difficult to teach, since the term "Truth" is used in the following different ways:

TRUTH, meaning GOD: GOD IS TRUTH.

TRUTH, meaning SANCTIFYING GRACE: GOD'S LOVE AND TRUTH IN US.

TRUTH, meaning DOCTRINE.

TRUTH, as opposed to what is false.

In Book Two the simple story "Tom and His Mother" presents in a childlike, interesting way TRUTH IN GOD, God's Truth in us, and truth in opposition to falsehood. Truth as doctrine is presented in a later lesson, through the story "God's Own Son, the Greatest and Holiest Teacher of Truth."

For, since the first story in Book Two teaches the important doctrine, GOD IS TRUTH, the last story of this book should logically be, "The Story about God's Own Son, Truth Itself Come to Earth." However, "A Story about God's Own Son Come to Earth" could not, either logically or psychologically, be told until it had been motivated by the presentation of "The Story of Our First Parents" and "The Doctrine of Original Sin" in such a clear, simple way that the child could understand it.

Then, as a link between the stories of "Our First Parents" and "The Coming to Earth of God's Own Son," there should, of course, be childlike stories concerning the Prophets.

The entire group of stories in Book Two is carefully designed to give to the child clear ideas concerning important doctrinal Truths; but, even more than this, these stories will, through the application of the principles of induction, motivation and self-activity bring about good training of the mind and the will.

These results have been obtained by those who have used the book properly in teaching the child. For the principle of self-activity inherent in this type of teaching causes him to become, spontaneously, an ardent apostle desirous of making others familiar with the doctrinal Truths which he himself has so well assimilated.

B. DOCTRINAL TRUTHS PRESENTED TO THE CHILD IN BOOK TWO WITH THE EXPECTATION THAT HE WILL UNDERSTAND AND APPRECIATE THEM IN ACCORDANCE WITH HIS MENTAL AGE:

That:

1. God is Truth;

2. God is the Great Giver of Truth;

3. God wants His Love and Truth in us (SANCTIFYING GRACE);

4. God wants us to love truth and to be truthful;

5. the father of the human race did not give to God love and obedience. He turned away from God;

6. after the father of the human family had turned away from God, he no longer shared in God's Love and Truth. He did not have God's blessing;

7. God had pity on our first parents, and promised to send Someone to live upon this earth Who would have the power to more than make up for the refusal of our first parents to give to Him the love and obedience they owed Him;

8. the prophets kept God's Great Promise alive in the minds of the people for centuries;

9. Adam was the head of the family, and had lost God's blessing for his family as well as for himself;

10. after the head of the family had turned away from God, none of his children would have God's Love and Truth in them at the beginning of their lives;

11. we do not have God's Love and Truth in us at the beginning of our lives and for this reason we are said to be born in the state of original sin;

12. God sent His Own Son to live upon the earth as we do so that we may know the One True God, and have His Love and Truth in us;

13. through Baptism we share in God's Love and Truth, and thus are made children of God;

14. we are holy when God gives us of HIS LOVE AND TRUTH, and, like Saint John the Baptist, when we are filled with God's Love and Truth we may be called "Saints";

15. we should show gratitude to God for HIS GOODNESS to us.

C. GROWTH IN POWER TO BE EXPECTED IN THE CHILD AS A RESULT OF STUDYING BOOK TWO

Greater facility:

1. in interpreting the printed page;
2. in giving oral expression to the interpreted thought;
3. in being truthful under difficult circumstances;
4. in appreciating his position as a child of Adam;
5. in realizing God's Mercy and Goodness to us;
6. in grasping the doctrine, "The Divinity of Christ";
7. in knowing and loving the God of Truth through His Own Beloved Son;
8. in praying with confidence;
9. in making his own Catechism Project Book.

D. PEDAGOGICAL STRUCTURE

When we are presenting a doctrinal truth in a way which is in harmony with the natural workings of the human mind, the truth will meet with a warmer reception than it otherwise would; more interest will be evoked, and therefore more spirituality developed.

And every conscientious teacher of religion should always keep in mind that the goal of good religious teaching is holiness.

The following outline presents the doctrinal principle "God Is Truth" in a way that is in harmony with the natural workings of the human mind.

Teacher's Major Objectives

To develop in the child-mind a further correct idea concerning the Nature of God, that is, God is All-Truth;

To develop in the child-mind correct ideas concerning the head of the human race, his turning away from God, that is, his refusal to give God love and obedience, and the effect of this refusal upon the human race;

To develop in the child-mind correct ideas concerning God's Promise and the way this Promise was kept alive in the minds of the chosen people;

To develop in the child-mind correct ideas concerning the Divinity of Jesus and His Mission.

Exploration and the Establishment of an Apperceptive Background for the New Knowledge

This part of the lesson is an exploration into the child's mind to discover what he already knows which would dovetail into the new subject-matter about to be presented and establish an appropriate apperceptive background for it.

a. The truth, GOD IS ALL-LOVE and THE GREAT GIVER OF LOVE, which was taught in Book One, is recalled.

b. In Essence God is All-Love and ALL-TRUTH. For balanced teaching concerning God, Book Two would necessarily teach that GOD IS ALL-TRUTH and THE GREAT GIVER OF TRUTH. In preparing an appropriate apperceptive background for the teaching of an abstract truth, either familiar knowledge bearing upon the topic must be recalled, or appropriate new knowledge which would provide a background must be given. The new knowledge, GOD IS ALL-TRUTH and THE GREAT GIVER OF TRUTH, is merely stated in the introduction instead of developed, because there are different concepts of truth, and the child must be made acquainted with these different concepts gradually.

c. In the story, "Tom and His Mother," the concept of truth as opposed to falsehood is within the child's experience, and is recalled.

After giving the child the new concept of God as TRUTH ITSELF and THE GREAT GIVER OF TRUTH, the added concept that God wants His Truth in us is given.

The teaching that God gives us of His Love and Truth is the foundation teaching for developing the definition of SANCTIFYING GRACE.

In the last paragraph on page 2 the three concepts of truth brought out in the story are united; that is, THE GOD OF TRUTH, GOD'S TRUTH IN US, and THE VIRTUE OF TRUTHFULNESS. The concept, TRUTH AS DOCTRINE, will be developed in later stories.

CONFIDENCE IN GOD THROUGH PRAYER is like a rock upon which the value of the story rests.

Motivation

a. In a child's book in which the beginning teaching is GOD IS ALL-TRUTH, the last story in the book would logically contain teaching CONCERNING THE COMING TO EARTH OF THE SECOND PERSON OF THE BLESSED TRINITY, the Wisdom of the Father, the Image of the Father, TRUTH ITSELF.

b. Teaching concerning the coming of the Second Person of the Blessed Trinity to earth to live as one of us, WOULD NECESSARILY BE MOTIVATED BY TEACHING CONCERNING THE FIRST MAN AND WOMAN, THEIR SIN and ORIGINAL SIN.

c. Further motivation would be included in the story, "A Promise by the God of Truth," and the prophecy of Isaias concerning the coming of a Child Who would be called Wonderful, the Prince of Peace. These motivating stories are told on pages 6 to 15.

d. On pages 16 and 17 further motivation is brought about by giving suggestions which would arouse the child's curiosity concerning THE POWER OF THIS CHILD and what He could do for us.

Presentation of New Knowledge

Page

a. God is All-Truth 2

b. God gives us of His Love and Truth at the time of our Baptism   2

c. 19-29

God's Own Son:

1. was expected by the Prophets; and Saint John the Baptist, the last of the Prophets, told the people to prepare for the coming of God's Own Son and urged them to do penance for their sins;

2. was baptized by Saint John the Baptist. "And Jesus being baptized forthwith came out of the water: and lo, the heavens were opened....And behold a voice from heaven, saying: THIS IS MY BELOVED SON in Whom I am well pleased";

3. came to live upon this earth to offer to His Father such great love and obedience that He would more than make up for the turning away from God of our first parents and all those who would come after them;

4. came to live in this world to teach Truth;

5. would have the power to give God's Love and Truth to the people;

6. knew that when He told the high priest Who He was He would be put to death;

7. was willing to be put to a cruel death so that all people to the end of the world WOULD BE SURE that He was the Son of God and that His teachings are true.

Generalizations

a. God is All-Love and All-Truth.

b. God loves Truth.

c. God is the Great Giver of Love and Truth. He gives us of His Love and Truth at the time of our Baptism.

d. Adam, the head of us all, failed to give God love and obedience.

e. Then our first parents no longer had God's Love and Truth in them, and none of their family would have God's Love and Truth in them.

f. God is All-Good and He had pity on our first parents. He made a Promise that a Child would be born Who would have the power to offer Him enough Love and Obedience to make up for the failure of Adam, the head of us all, and to find a way to give us of God's Love and Truth. God's Own Son was the Promised Child.

g. God's Own Son would be the Greatest Teacher of Truth the world would ever have.

Applications and Related Activities

E. THEOLOGICAL BACKGROUND

Bigness of outlook on the part of a religious teacher means that he is drawing from a deep and rugged source of doctrine which in turn will have its effect upon the minds of those he is teaching. And the effect on those minds will be good, giving them a better understanding of other minds, and thus enabling them to influence the society in which they live.

Narrowness of outlook on the part of the teacher often brings about pettiness and formalism in those being taught. And the effect is bad both for the individual and for the Church in general.

A foundation study of doctrine, as presented by the Doctors of the Church, is a source sure to give both a sound and a big outlook, a pearl which will bring happiness and joy to many.

The doctrine presented in this section gives some of the teachings of great theologians concerning the doctrine "God Is Truth."

1. Immutable Truth

a. "Hence thou must in no manner deny that there is an IMMUTABLE TRUTH, embracing all such things as are immutably true; a truth which thou canst not call thine, or mine, or any man's, but which is present to all and gives itself to all alike who discern the things that are immutably true, as a light which in some miraculous way is both secret and yet open to all. . . . "

St. Augustine, "De lib. arb.," II, XII, 33.

b. "Since it is in truth that we learn to know and to embrace the supreme good, and since that truth is wisdom, let us discern the supreme good in truth and embrace it and enjoy it to the full. For blessed is he who enjoys the supreme good. And this truth shows forth all good things that are truly good; and men understanding these choose, each according to his capacity, some one or more of these, for their enjoyment. For whatever in other true things is a cause of delight, must certainly give delight in THE TRUTH ITSELF. This is our freedom, to subject ourselves to that Truth, and He is our God who liberates us from death, that is from the state of sin."

Ibid., XIII, 36, 37.

c. "In every place, O TRUTH, thou givest audience to such as consult thee, and at the same time dost thou answer all their demands, be they never so diverse. Thou givest them clear answers, but everyone doth not clearly understand thee. For all men consult thee about what they will, but they do not always hear what they will by way of answer. He is thy best servant who endeavoreth not to hear that from thee which he desireth, but rather desireth that which he heareth from thee."

St. Augustine, "Conf.," X, XXVI, 37.

2. God Is Truth

a. "For if God is man's supreme good ... it clearly follows, since to seek the supreme good is to live well, that to live well is nothing else but to love God with all the heart, with all the soul, and with all the mind. ... This is man's one perfection, by which alone he can succeed in attaining to the PURITY OF TRUTH."
St. Augustine, "De Mor. Eccl.," I, XXV, 46.

b. "O ETERNAL TRUTH, and true Charity, and lovely Eternity! Thou art my God, to thee do I sigh day and night."
St. Augustine, "Conf.," VII, X, 16.

c. "I call upon Thee, O GOD, THE TRUTH, in Whom, by Whom and through Whom those things are true which are true in every respect. ... God, Whom to forsake is the same as to perish: Whom to strive for is the same as to live; Whom to see is the same as to possess. God, to Whom faith urges us, hope raises us, charity joins us."
St. Augustine, "Solil.," I, 1, 3.

d. "If, then, any intellect exists wherein there can be no alternation of opinions, and of which nothing can escape the knowledge, in this is immutable truth. Such is the Divine Intellect. Hence THE TRUTH OF THE DIVINE INTELLECT IS IMMUTABLE."
St. Thomas Aquinas, "Summa Theologica,"
Part One, First Number, Q. XVI, Art. VIII.

e. "The Divine Act of Intelligence is the very substance itself of the One Who understands."
Ibid., Second Number, Q. XXVII, Art. II.

f. "GOD'S INTELLECT IS HIS SUBSTANCE. ... Hence, as His Essence Itself is also His Intelligible Species, it necessarily follows that His Act of Understanding Itself must be His Essence and His Existence."
Ibid., Part One, First Number, Q. XIV, Art. IV.

g. "As God is His own very Existence and Intellect, so is He His own Life."
Ibid., Q. XVIII, Art. III.

h. "THE LIFE OF GOD IS HIS INTELLECT. In God, the Intellect, the thing understood, and the act of understanding are one and the same."
Ibid., Q. XVIII, Art. IV.

i. "Knowledge is not a quality in God nor a habit; but Substance and Pure Act."

Ibid., Q. XIV, Art. I.

j. "Since GOD has nothing in Him of potentiality, but IS PURE ACT, the Intellect and its object in Him are altogether the same."

Ibid., Art. II.

k. "The Species of the Divine Intellect, which is God's Essence, suffices to represent all things. Hence by understanding His Essence, God knows the essence of all things, and also whatever can be accidental to them."

Ibid., Art. XIV.

l. "Because only the Divine Intellect is eternal, in it alone TRUTH has eternity. Nor does it follow from this that anything else but God is eternal; since THE TRUTH OF THE DIVINE INTELLECT IS GOD HIMSELF."

Ibid., Q. XVI, Art. VII.

m. "TRUTH is found in the intellect according as it apprehends a thing as it is; and in things according as they have being conformable to the intellect. This is to the greatest degree found in God. His Being is not only conformed to His Intellect, but it is the very act of His Intellect Itself; and this is the measure and cause of every other being and every other intellect, and He Himself is His Own Existence and Intellect. Whence it follows that not only is TRUTH in Him, but that HE HIMSELF IS TRUTH ITSELF, AND THE SOVEREIGN AND FIRST TRUTH."

Ibid., Art. V.

n. " 'As from one face many likenesses are reflected in a mirror, so many truths are reflected from the one Divine Truth.' (St. Augustine). If we speak of truth as it exists in things, then ALL THINGS ARE TRUE BY ONE PRIMARY TRUTH; to which each one is assimilated according to its own entity. Thus, although the essences or forms of things are many, yet THE TRUTH OF THE DIVINE INTELLECT IS ONE, IN CONFORMITY TO WHICH ALL THINGS ARE SAID TO BE TRUE."

Ibid., Art. VI.

3. God Loves Truth

a. "Everything loves what is like to itself."
Ibid., First Number, Q. XX, Art. IV.

b. "God loves Christ (THE TRUTH) not only more than He loves the whole human race, but more than He loves the entire created universe."
Ibid., Art. IV.

c. "The Greek Fathers understand by the Truth, Christ Himself; meaning, Ye shall know Me to be the Truth, shadowed forth by the figures of the Old Law, from which I will set you free, that ye may serve God not with bodily ceremonies, but in the Spirit and Truth of faith, hope and charity."
Cornelius à Lapide (St. John 8:32).

d. "Christ says in the fourteenth chapter: 'I am the Way, the Truth, and the Life.' FOR IN CHRIST THERE IS ALL TRUTH, and that fourfold: there is the truth of being or existence, the truth of the soul, the truth of word, and the truth of deed.

"Truth lies hid, as the true Deity lay hid in the humanity of Christ. Yet it cannot lie hid forever.... Wherefore, the truth may be oppressed, but can never be extinguished; just as the sun may be obscured by the clouds, but by and by it disperses the clouds by the force of its rays, and shines out brightly. Such is truth, and such too is Christ."
Ibid. (St. John 1:4).

4. God Is the Great Giver of Love and Truth

a. "The word 'Gift' imports an appitude for being given. And what is given has an aptitude or relation both to the giver and to that to which it is given. For it would not be given by anyone, unless it was his to give.... Now a Divine Person is said to belong to another, either by origin, as the Son belongs to the Father; or as possessed by another. But we are said to possess what we can freely use or enjoy as we please: and in this way a Divine Person cannot be possessed, except by a rational creature united to God.... The rational creature does sometimes attain thereto; as when it is made partaker of the Divine Word and of the Love proceeding, so as freely to know truly and rightly to love God. Hence the rational creature alone can possess the Divine Person. Nevertheless in order that it may possess Him in this manner, its own power avails nothing: hence this must be given it from above; for that is said to be given to us which we have from another source. THUS A DIVINE PERSON CAN BE GIVEN, AND BE A GIFT."
St. Thomas Aquinas, op. cit.,
Part One, Second Number, Q. XXXVIII, Art. I.

b. "THE WHOLE TRINITY DWELLS IN THE MIND BY SANCTI-
FYING GRACE. . . . The soul is made like to God by grace. Hence
for a Divine Person to be sent to anyone by grace, there must needs be
a likening of the soul to the Divine Person Who is sent, by some gift
of grace. Because the Holy Ghost is Love, the soul is assimilated to
the Holy Ghost by the gift of charity: hence the mission of the Holy
Ghost is according to the mode of charity. Whereas the Son is the
Word, not any sort of word but One Who breathes forth Love. . . . If
we consider mission as regards the effect of grace, in that sense the two
missions [the Son and the Holy Ghost] are united in the root, which
is grace, but are distinguished in the effects of grace, which consist in
the illumination of the intellect and the kindling of the affections."

                                    Ibid., Q. XLIII, Art. V.

c. "We have a more perfect knowledge of God by grace than by natural
reason. . . . The intellect's natural light is strengthened by the infusion
of THE LIGHT OF GRACE."

                                    Ibid., First Number, Q. XII, Art. XIII.

d. "The created intellect cannot see the Essence of God, unless God by
His grace unites Himself to the created intellect, as an object made
intelligible to it."

                                    Ibid., Art. IV.

e. "It is necessary that some supernatural disposition should be added to
the intellect in order that it may be raised up to such a great and sublime height; since the natural power of the created intellect does not
avail to enable it to see the Essence of God, as was shown in the preceding article, it is necessary that the power of understanding should
be added by Divine Grace. This increase of the intellectual powers is
called the illumination of the intellect, as we also call the intelligible
object itself by the name of light or illumination. . . . By this light the
Blessed are made deiform — that is, like to God. . . . Hence the light
of glory can only be natural to a creature if the creature had a Divine
nature; which is impossible. BY THIS LIGHT THE RATIONAL
CREATURE IS MADE DEIFORM, as is said in this article."

                                    Ibid., Art. V.

5. God's Love and Truth Are in Us

a. "God is in anything in two ways: in one way as its active cause; and thus He is in all things created by Him; in another way He is in things as the object of operation is in the operator; and this belongs to the operations of the soul, according as the thing known is in the one who knows, and the thing desired in the one desiring. In this second way God is especially in the rational creature, which knows and loves Him actually or habitually. And because the rational creature possesses this prerogative by grace . . . He is said to be thus IN THE SAINTS BY GRACE."

Ibid., Q. VIII, Art. III.

b. "Under the word GRACE here include TRUTH also. For Christ is spoken of as FULL OF GRACE AND TRUTH. AND OF HIS FUL-NESS of both HAVE WE ALL RECEIVED. For through Christ have we received TRUTH, that is knowledge of God, faith, wisdom, understanding of salvation and things Divine: also remission of sins, reconciliation with God, the adoption of sons, charity, humility, and all other virtues and gifts. All are here comprehended under the word grace."

Cornelius à Lapide (St. John 1:6-16).

c. "The voice only strikes upon the outward ears, but Christ, by His grace, both strikes upon and illuminates the soul."

Ibid. (1:4).

6. God Wants All of His Children to Keep His Love and Truth in Them

a. "It is due to God that there should be fulfilled in creatures what His Will and Wisdom require; and what manifests His Goodness."

St. Thomas Aquinas, loc. cit., Q. XXI, Art. I

7. Prayer

a. "Prayer is offered to a person in two ways: first as to be fulfilled by him, secondly as to be obtained through him. In the first way we offer prayer to God alone, since ALL OUR PRAYERS OUGHT TO BE DIRECTED TO THE ACQUISITION OF GRACE AND GLORY, which God alone gives, according to Psalm 83:12: 'The Lord will give grace and glory.'"

Ibid., Part Two, Second Part, Q. LXXXIII, Art. IV.

b. "The Lord is said to hear the desire of the poor, either because desire is the cause of their petition, since a petition is like the interpreter of a desire, or in order to show how speedily they are heard, since no sooner do the poor desire something than God hears them before they put up a prayer."

Ibid., Art. I.

c. "By praying, man surrenders his mind to God, since he subjects it to Him with reverence, and so to speak, presents it to Him. . . . Wherefore just as the human mind excels exterior things, whether bodily members, or those external things that are employed for God's service, so too, PRAYER SURPASSES OTHER ACTS OF RELIGION."

Ibid., Art. III.

d. "Although man cannot by himself know what he ought to pray for, THE SPIRIT, as stated in the same passage, helpeth our infirmity, since by inspiring us with holy desires He MAKES US ASK FOR WHAT IS RIGHT. Hence our Lord said (John 4:24) that true adorers must adore . . . in spirit and in truth."

Ibid., Art. V.

e. " . . . When we pray we ought to ask for what we ought to desire. Now we ought to desire good things, not only for ourselves but also for others: for this is essential to the love which we owe our neighbor."

Ibid., Art. VII.

f. "Individual prayer is that which is offered by any single person, whether he pray for himself or for others; and it is not essential to such a prayer as this that it be vocal. . . . The voice is used in praying as though to pay a debt, so that man may serve God with all that he has from God, that is to say, not only with his mind but also with his body. . . . Vocal prayer is employed, not in order to tell God something He does not know, but in order to lift up the mind of the person praying or of other persons to God."

Ibid., Art. XII.

8. Man Was Constituted in Grace

a. "Man and angel are both ordained to grace. But the angels were created in grace, for Augustine says God at the same time fashioned their nature and endowed them with grace. Therefore man also was created in grace. . . . In the opinion of some, man was not created in grace; which was nevertheless bestowed on him subsequently before sin, for many authorities of the saints confess that man possessed grace in the state of innocence. But the very rectitude of the primitive state wherewith man was endowed by God seems to require that, as others say, he was created in grace, according to Ecclesiastes 7:30: 'GOD MADE MAN RIGHT.' For this rectitude consisted in his reason being subject to God, the lower powers to reason and the body to the soul."

Ibid.,
Part One, Third Number, Q. XCV, Art. I.

b. "Now it is clear that such a subjection of the body to the soul and of the lower powers to reason, was not from nature; otherwise it would have remained after sin; since even in the demons the natural gifts remained after sin, as Dionysius declares ('Div. Nom.,' IV). So it is clear also that the primitive subjection by virtue of which reason was subject to God, was not a merely natural gift, but was a supernatural endowment of grace; for it is not possible that the effect should be of greater efficiency than the cause. Hence Augustine says ('De Civ. Dei,' XIII) that, as soon as they disobeyed the Divine Command, and forfeited Divine grace, they were ashamed of their nakedness, for they felt the impulse of disobedience in the flesh, as though it were a punishment corresponding to their own disobedience. Hence if the loss of grace dissolved the obedience of the flesh to the soul, we may gather that the inferior powers were subjected to the soul through grace existing therein."

Ibid.

c. "We merit glory by an act of grace; but we do not merit grace by an act of nature."

Ibid.

9. The Sin of Our First Parents
and Its Sad Results for Them

a. "Man's disobedience to the Divine Command was not willed by man
for its own sake, for this could not happen unless one presupposes in-
ordinateness in his will. It remains therefore that he willed it for the
sake of something else. Now the first thing he coveted inordinately
was his own excellence; and consequently his disobedience was the
result of his pride. This agrees with the statement of Augustine who
says to Orosius ('Dial.,' Q. LXV, 4) that 'man puffed up with his
pride obeyed the serpent's prompting, and scorned God's commands.'

"Gluttony also had a place in the sin of our first parents ... yet
the very goodness and beauty of the fruit was not their first motive
for sinning, but the persuasive words of the serpent who said, 'Your
eyes shall be opened and you shall be as Gods'; and it was by coveting
this that the woman fell into pride. Hence the sin of gluttony resulted
from the sin of pride. . . . She believed the demon to have spoken truly."

Ibid.,
Part Two, Second Part, Q. CLXIII, Art. I.

b. "They were punished in two ways. In the first place by being deprived
of that which was befitting the state of integrity, namely, the place of
the earthly paradise. . . . Secondly, they were punished by having appointed to them things befitting a nature bereft of the aforesaid favor:
and this as regards both the body and the soul. With regard to the
body, to which pertains the distinction of sex, one punishment was
appointed to the woman and another to the man. . . . Likewise a triple
punishment is ascribed to them on the part of the soul: first, by reason
of the confusion they experienced at the rebellion of the flesh against
the spirit; . . . secondly, by the reproach of their sin; . . . thirdly, by the
reminder of their coming death. . . . "

Ibid., Q. CLXIV, Art. II.

c. "Paradise, as Isidore says ('Etymol.,' XIV), is a place situated in the
east, the name being Greek for garden."

Ibid., Part One, Third Number, Q. CII, Art. I.

10. The Doctrine of Original Sin

a. "Original sin in Adam, which is a sin of the nature, is derived from his actual sin, which is a personal sin, because in him the person corrupted the nature; and by means of this corruption the sin of the first man is transmitted to posterity, inasmuch as the corrupt nature corrupts the person. Now grace is not vouchsafed us by means of human nature, but solely by the personal action of Christ Himself. Hence we must not distinguish a twofold grace in Christ, one corresponding to the nature, the other to the person, as in Adam we distinguish the sin of the nature and the person."

Ibid.,
Part Three, First Number, Q. VIII, Art. V.

b. "And in the hope wherein we hope that we shall adhere to the contemplation of the Truth, we are meanwhile made subject to vanity. For all creation, spiritual, animal and bodily, is in man; indeed is man. It sinned of its own free will, AND BECAME AN ENEMY TO TRUTH; but that it might justly be punished, it was not of its own free will made subject to vanity.... As long as we are here according to the flesh, whose adoption and redemption we here wait for in the patience of hope, so long, in that respect in which we are under the sun, we are made subject to vanity."

St. Augustine, "In Ps. CXVIII, Serm. XII," 1.

c. "Children contract original sin from the sin of Adam; which is made clear by the fact that they are under the ban of death, which PASSED UPON ALL on account of the sin of the first man.... Consequently it became necessary to baptize children, that as in birth they incurred damnation through Adam, so IN A SECOND BIRTH THEY MIGHT OBTAIN SALVATION THROUGH CHRIST."

St. Thomas Aquinas, loc. cit.,
Third Number, Q. LXVIII, Art. IX.

d. "It is manifest that in carnal generation man does not beget in respect of his soul, but in respect of his body. Consequently the children of those who are baptized are born with original sin; wherefore they need to be baptized."

Ibid., Art. I.

e. "Baptism is conferred principally as a remedy against original sin. Wherefore, just as original sin is not renewed, so neither is Baptism reiterated."

Ibid., Q. LXVI, Art. IX.

11. God Gave His Grace to Those Holy People Living under the Old Law Who Believed in Him and His Promises and Obeyed His Law

a. "Before Christ's coming, men were incorporated in Christ by faith in His future coming: of which faith, circumcision was the seal . . . whereas before circumcision was instituted men were INCORPORATED IN CHRIST BY FAITH ALONE. . . . Again, since Christ's coming, men are incorporated in Christ by faith. . . . But a faith in a thing already present is manifested by a sign different from that by which it was manifested when that thing was yet in the future. . . . Consequently, although the Sacrament itself of Baptism was not always necessary for salvation, yet FAITH, OF WHICH BAPTISM IS THE SACRAMENT, WAS ALWAYS NECESSARY."

Ibid., Q. LXVIII, Art. I.

12. The Word, Truth Itself, God's Own Son, Came upon This Earth to Teach the People to Know, to Love and to Serve the One True God; to Restore the Order of Justice; and to Establish a Way through Which All People May Have God's Love and Truth in Them

a. "Nothing belonging to the intellect can be applied to God personally, except 'Word' alone; for 'Word' alone signifies what proceeds from another. For what the intellect forms in its conception is the word."

Ibid., Part One, Second Number, Q. XXXIV, Art. I.

b. "So in this manner the procession of the Word in God is generation; for He proceeds by way of intelligible action which is a vital operation: and exists in the same nature, because in God the act of understanding and His existence are the same. Hence the procession of the Word in God is called generation; and the Word Himself proceeding is called the Son."

Ibid., Q. XXVII, Art. II.

c. "Now WORD is taken strictly in God, as signifying the concept of the intellect. Hence Augustine says: 'Whoever can understand the word, not only before it is sounded, but also before thought has clothed it with imaginary sound, can already see some likeness of that Word of Whom it is said: IN THE BEGINNING WAS THE WORD.' "

Ibid., Q. XXXIV, Art. I.

d. "Therefore when we say that WORD is knowledge, the term 'knowledge' does not mean the act of knowing intellect, or any one of its habits, but stands for what the intellect conceives by knowing. Hence also Augustine says that THE WORD IS BEGOTTEN WISDOM."

Ibid.

e. "The Divine Person can be manifested in a twofold manner by the essential attributes; in one way by similitude, and thus THE THINGS WHICH BELONG TO THE INTELLECT ARE APPROPRIATED TO THE SON, WHO PROCEEDS BY WAY OF INTELLECT, AS WORD.... The Son is called the Wisdom of the Father, because He is Wisdom from the Father Who is Wisdom. For each of them is of Himself Wisdom, and both together are one Wisdom."

Ibid., Q. XXXIX, Art. VII.

f. "We can say that since TRUTH belongs to the intellect it is appropriated to the Son without however being a property of His."

Ibid., Art. VIII.

g. "Wherefore there can be but one Person proceeding after the manner of Word, which Person is the Son."

Ibid., Q. XLI, Art. VI.

h. "Whence, as He is the only true and natural Son of God, He is called the only-begotten according to the text ... (John 1:18), and so far as OTHERS ARE ENTITLED SONS OF ADOPTION BY THEIR SIMILITUDE TO HIM, He is called the first-begotten, according to the words of Romans 8:29."

Ibid., Art. III.

i. "IT BELONGS TO HIM [JESUS], AS MAN, TO UNITE MEN TO GOD, by communicating to men both precepts and gifts, and by offering satisfaction and prayer to God for men.... Although IT BELONGS TO CHRIST AS GOD TO TAKE AWAY SIN AUTHORITATIVELY, YET IT BELONGS TO HIM, AS MAN, TO SATISFY FOR THE SIN OF THE HUMAN RACE."

Ibid., Part Three, First Number, Q. XXVI, Art. II.

j. "Christ did not slay Himself, but OF HIS OWN FREE WILL HE EXPOSED HIMSELF TO DEATH, according to Isaias 53:7: 'He was offered because it was His own will.' Thus He is said to have offered Himself."

Ibid., Q. XXII, Art. II.

k. " 'Behold...Him Who taketh away the sin of the world.' By SIN here is to be understood the first and universal sin of Adam, that is, original sin, which he by generation transmitted to all his posterity, and out of which all actual sins, whether venial or mortal, spring. Christ therefore, in taking away sin, takes away its source as well as its filth."

Cornelius à Lapide (St. John 1:29).

l. "You may say, it would have been greater love if God the Father had given Himself for us, and taken our flesh, than that He sent His Son. For he gives more who gives himself than he who sends another. But I reply that this is true of those who are of a different essence, but not of God: for the Father and the Son have the same Divine Essence, and are consubstantial. WHEREFORE THE FATHER, IN GIVING US HIS SON, WITH HIM GAVE US HIS OWN ESSENCE, THAN WHICH NOTHING GREATER CAN EXIST, OR BE GIVEN."

Ibid. (3:16).

m. "Son of God:...The meaning is, we believe that Thou art the Son of God. WHEREFORE, WE ALSO BELIEVE THAT ALL THY SAYINGS ARE DIVINE AND MOST TRUE, EVEN WHEN WE DO NOT UNDERSTAND THEM, AND THEREFORE THAT THEY ARE LIFE-GIVING, AND CONFER SALVATION AND ETERNAL LIFE. For Thou art the Son of the Living God, Who in His Essence is Life, which He communicates to Thee: therefore nothing can proceed from Thee but what is vital and life-giving: neither do we expect anything else from Thee."

Ibid. (6:70).

F. BIBLICAL BACKGROUND

A teacher who studies the inspired Word of God concerning any doctrine will surely develop a bigness and richness of outlook which necessarily will give a quality of depth and power to the teaching of this doctrine.

Consequently anyone who is offering his teaching endeavor to God as an apostolate should always strive to know some texts from the Bible which will illuminate the doctrine to be taught.

The following is a Biblical background which will give bigness and richness to the teaching of the doctrine contained in the book, "God Is Truth."

1. The God of Truth

a. Psalm 25:3

"... I am well pleased with Thy TRUTH."

Psalm 30:6

"... Thou hast redeemed me, O Lord, THE GOD OF TRUTH."

Psalm 35:6

"... O Lord, Thy mercy is in heaven and THY TRUTH reacheth even to the clouds."

Psalm 39:12

"... Thy mercy and THY TRUTH have always upheld me."

Psalm 42:3

"Send forth Thy light and THY TRUTH: they have conducted me and brought me unto Thy holy hill, and into Thy tabernacles."

Psalm 56:11

"For thy mercy is magnified even to the heavens: and Thy TRUTH unto the clouds."

Psalm 60:8

"His mercy and TRUTH who shall search?"

Psalm 85:11

"Conduct me, O Lord, in Thy way and I will walk in Thy TRUTH...."

Psalm 88:2, 3

"I will show forth Thy TRUTH with my mouth to generation and generation.... Mercy shall be built up forever in the heavens; Thy TRUTH shall be prepared in them."

Psalm 88:9, 15

"... Thou art mighty, O Lord, and Thy TRUTH is round about Thee.... Mercy and TRUTH shall go before Thy face."

Psalm 90:5

"His TRUTH shall compass thee with a shield: thou shalt not be afraid of the terror of the night."

Psalm 99:4, 5

"Praise ye His name: for the Lord is sweet, His mercy endureth forever, and His TRUTH to generation and generation."

Psalm 116:2

"... The TRUTH of the Lord remaineth forever."

Psalm 118:89, 90

"Forever, O Lord, Thy word standeth firm in heaven; Thy TRUTH unto all generations...."

b. John 3:33

"He that hath received His testimony hath set to his seal that God is TRUE."

c. Romans 3:4

"But God is TRUE."

d. 1 John 2:27

"... His unction teacheth you of all things, and is TRUTH, and is no lie. And as it hath taught you, abide in Him."

2. God Loves Truth

a. Psalm 50:8

"For behold, Thou hast loved TRUTH...."

Psalm 83:12

"For God loveth mercy and TRUTH: the Lord will give grace and glory."

Psalm 144:18

"The Lord is nigh unto all them that call upon Him: to all that call upon Him in TRUTH."

3. God's Truth in Us

a. Psalm 14:1,3

"Lord, who shall dwell in Thy tabernacle? or who shall rest in Thy holy hill? He that speaketh TRUTH in his heart: who hath not used deceit in his tongue."

Psalm 30:24

"O love the Lord ... for the Lord will require TRUTH."

Psalm 56:5

"God hath sent His mercy and His TRUTH, and He hath delivered my SOUL."

b. Proverbs 3:3, 4

"Let not mercy and TRUTH leave thee, put them about thy neck, and write them in the tables of thy heart: and thou shalt find grace and good understanding before God and men."

Proverbs 14:22

"Mercy and TRUTH prepare good things."

c. Ecclesiasticus 15:8

" . . . Men that speak TRUTH shall be found with her [wisdom] and shall advance even till they come to the sight of God."

d. Isaias 26:2

"Open ye the gates and let the just nation that keepeth the TRUTH, enter in."

e. John 17:17

"Sanctify them in TRUTH."

f. 2 Corinthians 11:10

"The TRUTH of Christ is in me. . . . "

g. Ephesians 4:24

"And put on the new man, who according to God is created in justice and holiness of TRUTH."

Ephesians 5:8, 9

"Walk then as children of the light. For the fruit of the light is in all goodness and justice and TRUTH."

Ephesians 6:14

"Stand therefore having your loins girt about with TRUTH."

h. 2 John 1:1, 2, 4

"The ancient to the lady Elect, and her children, whom I love in the TRUTH. . . . For the sake of THE TRUTH WHICH DWELLETH IN US and shall be with us forever. I was exceeding glad that I found of thy children walking in TRUTH as we have received a commandment from the Father."

i. 3 John 1:3, 4

"I was exceedingly glad when the brethren came and gave testimony to the TRUTH IN THEE, even as thou walkest in the TRUTH. I have no greater grace than this, to hear that my children walk in TRUTH."

4. When God's Truth Is Not in Us

a. 2 Thessalonians 2:10

" . . . Because they received NOT THE LOVE OF THE TRUTH, that they might be saved. Therefore God shall send them the operation of error to believe lying."

b. I Timothy 6:5

" . . . Conflicts of men corrupted in mind and who are DESTITUTE OF THE TRUTH, supposing gain to be godliness."

c. I John 1:8

"If we say that we have no sin, we deceive ourselves, and THE TRUTH IS NOT IN US."

I John 2:4

"He who saith that he knoweth Him and keepeth not His commandments is a liar, and THE TRUTH IS NOT IN HIM."

5. Truth As Doctrine

a. John 8:32

"And you shall know the TRUTH, and the TRUTH shall make you free."

John 17:17

"Thy word is TRUTH."

b. Romans 1:24, 25

"Wherefore God gave them up to the desires of their heart. . . . Who changed the TRUTH of God into a lie."

c. 2 Corinthians 4:2

"But we renounce the hidden things of dishonesty, not walking in craftiness, nor adulterating the word of God; but by manifestation of the TRUTH commending ourselves to every man's conscience, in the sight of God."

2 Corinthians 6:4, 7

"But in all things let us exhibit ourselves as the ministers of God. . . . In the word of TRUTH, in the power of God."

d. Colossians 1:5

"For the hope that is laid up for you in heaven, which you have heard in the word of the TRUTH of the Gospel."

e. 2 Timothy 2:15

"Carefully study to present thyself approved unto God, a workman that needeth not to be ashamed, rightly handling the word of TRUTH."

2 Timothy 3:8

"Now as Jannes and Mambres resisted Moses, so these also resist the TRUTH, men corrupted in mind, reprobate concerning the faith."

2 Timothy 4:3, 4

"For there shall be a time when they will not endure sound doctrine;... and will indeed turn away their hearing from the TRUTH."

f. James 1:18

"For of His own will hath He begotten us by the word of TRUTH, that we might be some beginning of His creature."

g. 1 John 2:21

"I have not written to you as to them that know not the TRUTH, but as to them that know it."

6.   Truth versus Falsehood

a. Psalm 33:13, 14

"Who is the man that desireth life?...Keep thy tongue from evil, and thy lips from speaking guile."

b. Proverbs 12:17

"He that speaketh that which he knoweth, showeth forth justice: but he that lieth is a deceitful witness."

Proverbs 12:19

"The lip of TRUTH shall be steadfast forever; but he that is a hasty witness frameth a lying tongue."

c. Ecclesiasticus 4:24, 25

"...Be not ashamed to say the TRUTH. For there is a shame that bringeth sin."

Ecclesiasticus 27:10

"Birds resort unto their like: so TRUTH will return to them that practise her."

d. Isaias 59:14, 15

"... TRUTH hath fallen down in the street, and equity could not come in. And TRUTH hath been forgotten ... and the Lord saw and it appeared evil in His eyes."

e. Zacharias 8:16

"Speak ye TRUTH every one to his neighbor. ... "

Zacharias 8:19

"... only love ye TRUTH and peace."

f. John 8:44

"You are of your father the devil. ... He was a murderer from the beginning, and he stood not in the TRUTH; because the TRUTH is not in him. When he speaketh a lie, he speaketh of his own: for he is a liar and the father thereof."

g. James 3:14

"... Be not liars against the TRUTH."

h. I John 2:21

"... No lie is of the TRUTH."

i. Apocalypse 21:8

"But the fearful and unbelieving, and the abnominable ... and all liars, they shall have their portion in the pool burning with fire and brimstone, which is the second death."

7. Our First Parents

a. Genesis 1:26-28

"Let Us make man to Our image and likeness. ... AND GOD CREATED MAN TO HIS OWN IMAGE: to the image of God He created him. ... And God blessed them. ... "

Genesis 2:7

"And the Lord God formed man of the slime of the earth: and breathed into his face the breath of life and MAN BECAME A LIVING SOUL."

Genesis 2:15

"And the Lord God took man, and put him into the paradise of pleasure, to dress it and to keep it."

Genesis 2:21-23

"Then the Lord God cast a deep sleep upon Adam: and when he was fast asleep, he took one of his ribs. . . . And the Lord God built the rib which he took from Adam into a woman and brought her to Adam."

"And Adam said: This now is bone of my bones, and flesh of my flesh; SHE SHALL BE CALLED WOMAN because she was taken out of man."

Genesis 3:1-24

"Now the serpent was more subtle than any of the beasts of the earth which the Lord God had made. . . . And He cast out Adam; and placed before the paradise of pleasure cherubims and a flaming sword. . . . "

Genesis 5:1-5

"This is the book of the generation of Adam. . . . And all the time that Adam lived came to nine hundred and thirty years and he died."

b. Ecclesiasticus 17:1-13

"God created man of the earth, and made him after HIS OWN IMAGE. . . . Their ways are always before Him, they are not hidden from His eyes."

c. Romans 5:12

"Wherefore as by one man sin entered into this world, and by sin death; and so death passed upon all men, in whom all have sinned."

d. I Corinthians 11:3, 8, 12

"But I would have you know, that THE HEAD OF EVERY MAN IS CHRIST; and the head of the woman is the man; and the head of Christ is God. . . . For the man is not of the woman, but the woman of the man. . . . For as the woman is of the man so also is the man by the woman: but all things of God."

e. I Timothy 2:13, 15

"For Adam was first formed; then Eve. . . . Yet she shall be saved through childbearing; if she continue in faith, and love, and sanctification, with sobriety."

8. Original Sin

a. Genesis 8:21

"... For the imagination and thought of man's heart are prone to evil from his youth...."

b. Psalm 50:7

"For behold I was conceived in iniquities and in sins did my mother conceive me."

c. Job 14:4

"Who can make him clean that is conceived of unclean seed? Is it not Thou who only art?"

d. Ephesians 2:3

"... We ... were by nature children of wrath...."

9. People Who Did Not Have God's Love and Truth in Them

a. Genesis 6:5-7

"And God, seeing that THE WICKEDNESS OF MEN WAS GREAT on the earth, and that all the thought of their heart was bent upon evil at all times; it repented Him that He had made man on the earth. And being touched inwardly with sorrow of heart, He said: I will destroy man whom I have created from the face of the earth; ..."

Genesis 18:26

"And the Lord said to him: If I find in Sodom fifty just within the city, I will spare the whole place for their sake."

Genesis 19:1, 12, 13

"And two angels came to Sodom in the evening ... and they said to Lot.... We will destroy this place, because their cry is grown loud before the Lord Who hath sent us to destroy them."

b. Numbers 21:5, 6

"And SPEAKING AGAINST GOD AND MOSES.... Wherefore the Lord sent among the people fiery serpents which bit them and killed many of them."

c. I Kings 28:16-18

"And Samuel said: Why asketh thou me, seeing the Lord has departed from thee.... For the Lord will do to thee as He spoke by me, and He will rend thy kingdom out of thy hand.... BECAUSE THOU DIDST NOT OBEY THE VOICE OF THE LORD, neither didst thou execute the wrath of His indignation upon Amalec. Therefore hath the Lord done to thee what thou sufferest this day."

10.   God Knows All Things

a. Psalm 138:1-12

"Lord . . . Thou hast understood my thoughts afar off. . . . And Thou hast foreseen all my ways. . . . Behold, O Lord, Thou hast known all things, the last and those of old. . . . Thy knowledge is become wonderful to me: it is high, and I cannot reach to it."

b. Proverbs 15:3

"The eyes of the Lord in every place behold the good and the evil."

c. Ecclesiasticus 23:29

"For all things were known to the Lord God, before they were created: so also after they were perfected, He beholdeth all things."

Ecclesiasticus 42:19

"For the Lord knoweth all knowledge . . . and revealeth the traces of hidden things."

d. Jeremias 23:24

"Shall a man be hid in secret places, and I not see him, saith the Lord? Do not I fill heaven and earth, saith the Lord?"

e. Daniel 2:22

"He revealeth deep and hidden things, and knoweth what is in darkness and light is with Him."

Daniel 13:42, 43

"O eternal God, Who knowest hidden things, Who knowest all things before they come to pass, Thou knowest that they have borne false witness against me."

f. I John 3:20

" . . . God . . . knoweth all things."

11.   Prayer

a. Numbers 16:48

"And standing between the dead and the living, he [Aaron] prayed for the people, and the plague ceased."

b. Tobias 12:8

"Prayer is good . . . more than to lay up treasures of gold."

c. Psalm 76:2, 3
"I cried to the Lord with my voice . . . and He gave ear to me. In the day of my trouble I sought God . . . and I was not deceived."

Psalm 106:19
"And they cried to the Lord in their affliction: and He delivered them out of their distresses."

Psalm 140:2
"Let my prayer be directed as incense in Thy sight; the lifting up of my hands as evening sacrifice."

Psalm 141:3
"In His sight I pour out my prayer, and before Him I declare my trouble."

d. Baruch 4:21
"Be of good comfort, my children, cry to the Lord, and He will deliver you out of the hand of the princes, your enemies."

e. Matthew 7:11
"If you then, being evil, know how to give good gifts to your children: how much more will your Father Who is in heaven give good things to them that ask Him?"

f. Romans 12:12
"Rejoicing in hope. Patient in tribulation. Instant in prayer."

g. Colossians 4:2
"Be instant in prayer: watching in it with thanksgiving."

12. The Prophets

"The prophets of the Old Testament were extraordinary ambassadors of God, whose inspired preaching, wonderful works, and prophecies concerning the promised Redeemer, kept alive the faith of the people and their leaders and led them on to their sublime vocation" (Messmer).

Moses and David were great prophets, and many prophecies concerning the Redeemer are found in the Pentateuch and the Psalms.

Sixteen of the prophets are usually classified as the Major and the Minor Prophets.

13. St. John the Baptist

a. Matthew 3:1-14

"And in those days cometh JOHN THE BAPTIST preaching in the desert of Judea.... But John staying Him said: I ought to be baptized by Thee, and comest Thou to me?"

Matthew 11:2-11

"Now when John had heard in prison the works of Christ: sending two of his disciples he said to Him: Art Thou He that art to come or look we for another?... AMEN I SAY TO YOU, THERE HATH NOT RISEN AMONG THEM THAT ARE BORN OF WOMEN A GREATER THAN JOHN THE BAPTIST."

Matthew 14:1-12

"At that time Herod ... said to his servants: This is John the Baptist: he is risen from the dead. ... For Herod had put him into prison ... and beheaded John in the prison ... and his disciples came and took the body, and buried it and came and told Jesus."

Matthew 21:24-26

"Jesus said to them: . . . The baptism of John, whence was it? from heaven or from men? But they thought within themselves saying: . . . If we shall say, from men, we are afraid of the multitude; for all held John as a PROPHET."

b. Mark 1:2, 3

"As it is written in Isaias the prophet: BEHOLD I SEND MY ANGEL BEFORE THY FACE, WHO SHALL PREPARE THE WAY BEFORE THEE. A VOICE OF ONE CRYING IN THE DESERT: PREPARE YE THE WAY OF THE LORD, MAKE STRAIGHT HIS PATHS. . . . "

Mark 6:14-16

"And King Herod heard . . . and he said: John the Baptist is risen again from the dead. . . . John whom I beheaded he is risen again from the dead. . . . "

c. Luke 1:5-25

"There was in the days of Herod, the king of Judea, a certain priest named Zachary. . . . The angel said to him: . . . Thy wife Elizabeth shall bear thee a son and thou shalt call his name John."

Luke 1:41

"And it came to pass that when Elizabeth heard the salutation of Mary, THE INFANT LEAPED IN HER WOMB. And Elizabeth was filled with the Holy Ghost."

Luke 1:57-66

"Now Elizabeth's full time of being delivered was come, and she brought forth a son. . . . WHAT AN ONE, THINK YE, SHALL THIS CHILD BE? FOR THE HAND OF THE LORD WAS WITH HIM."

d. John 1:19-36

"And this is the testimony of John. . . . And beholding Jesus walking HE SAITH: Behold the Lamb of God."

John 3:23-36

"And John also was baptizing in Ennon near Salim. . . . You yourselves do bear me witness that I said, I AM NOT CHRIST BUT THAT I AM SENT BEFORE HIM. . . . He that believeth in the Son hath life everlasting."

John 5:32, 33

" . . . And I know that the witness which he witnesseth of Me is true. You sent to John, and HE GAVE TESTIMONY TO THE TRUTH."

14. God's Own Son

a. Genesis 3:15

"I will put enmities between thee and the woman, AND THY SEED AND HER SEED: she shall crush thy head, and thou shalt lie in wait for her heel."

b. Psalm 84:7-12

"Thou wilt turn, O God, and bring us to life. . . . Mercy and truth have met each other: justice and peace have kissed. TRUTH is sprung out of the earth."

c. Isaias 9:6

"For A CHILD IS BORN TO US, and a Son is given to us, and the government is upon His shoulder: and His name shall be called Wonderful, Counsellor, God the Mighty, the Father of the world to come, the Prince of Peace."

Isaias 35:4, 5

"Say to the fainthearted: Take courage, and fear not: behold your God will bring the revenge of recompense; God Himself will come and will save you. Then shall the eyes of the blind be opened, and the ears of the deaf shall be unstopped."

d. Joel 2:23

" . . . Be joyful in the Lord your God: because He hath given you a TEACHER OF JUSTICE."

e. Matthew 3:17

"And behold a voice from heaven saying: This is My beloved Son, in Whom I am well pleased."

Matthew 5:1, 2

" . . . His disciples came unto Him, and opening His mouth, He taught them. . . . "

Matthew 7:29

" . . . He [Jesus] was teaching them as one having power. . . . "

Matthew 16:16

"Simon Peter answered and said: THOU ART CHRIST, THE SON OF THE LIVING GOD."

f. Mark 14:61, 62

"... Again the high priest asked Him, and said to Him: Art Thou the Christ the Son of the blessed God? And Jesus said to him: I AM."

g. Luke 4:31, 32

"And He went down into Capharnaum ... and there He taught them. ... And they were astonished at His doctrine: for his speech was with power."

h. John 1:1-17

"In the beginning was the Word. ... And the Word was made flesh, and dwelt amongst us, and we saw His glory, the glory as it were of the Only-begotten of the Father, full of GRACE and TRUTH. ... For the Law was given by Moses; GRACE and TRUTH came by Jesus Christ."

John 3:16

"For God so loved the world, as to give HIS ONLY-BEGOTTEN SON."

John 5:18

"... The Jews sought ... to kill Him, because He ... said God was His Father. ... "

John 5:46

"For if you did believe Moses you would perhaps believe Me also; for he wrote of Me."

John 8:37-40

"... You seek to kill Me, because My word hath no place in you. I speak that which I have seen with My Father. ... But now you seek to kill Me, a Man WHO HAVE SPOKEN THE TRUTH TO YOU which I have heard of God."

John 10:30

"I and the Father are one."

John 14:6, 7, 13

"Jesus saith to him: I am the way, and the truth, and the life. No man cometh to the Father, but by Me. If you had known Me, you would without doubt have known My Father also. ... And whatsoever you shall ask the Father in My name, that will I do; that the Father may be glorified in the Son."

John 16:15
"All things whatsoever the Father hath are Mine."

John 18:37
"For this was I born and for this came I into the world; THAT I SHOULD GIVE TESTIMONY TO THE TRUTH. Everyone that is of the TRUTH heareth My voice."

i. Acts 10:43
"To Him [Jesus] all the prophets give testimony that by His name all receive remission of sins, who believe in Him."

Acts 28:23
"... There came very many to him [Paul] unto his lodgings; to whom he expounded, testifying the kingdom of God, and persuading them concerning Jesus out of the law of Moses and the prophets, from morning until evening."

j. Romans 5:15-19
"... For if by the offense of one, many died; much more the grace of God and the gift, by the grace of one Man, Jesus Christ, hath abounded unto many. . . . For as by the disobedience of one man many were made sinners; so also by the obedience of one, many shall be made just."

Romans 9:5
"... Of whom is Christ, according to the flesh, Who is over all things, God blessed forever."

k. I Corinthians 15:21, 22, 47
"For by a man came death and by a Man the resurrection of the dead. And as in Adam all die, so also in Christ all shall be made alive. . . . The first man was of the earth earthly; the second Man from heaven heavenly."

l. Ephesians 4:20, 21
"But ye have not so learned Christ, for in sooth ye have heard tell of Him and in Him ye have been instructed, as in Jesus is TRUTH" (Westminster).

m. Philippians 2:6
"Who being in the form of God thought it not robbery to be equal with God."

n. Hebrews 1:1-8

"God, Who ... spoke in times past to the fathers by the prophets, last of all ... hath spoken to us by His Son, Whom He hath appointed Heir of all things, by Whom also He made the world. ... For to which of the angels hath He said at any time, Thou art My Son, today have I begotten Thee? And again, I will be to Him a Father, and He shall be to Me a Son? And again ... Let all the angels of God adore Him. And ... He saith ... to the Son: Thy throne, O God, is forever and ever: a sceptre of justice is the sceptre of Thy kingdom."

o. 1 John 3:16

"In this we have known the charity of God, because He hath laid down His life for us."

1 John 4:9

" ... God hath sent His only-begotten Son into the world that we may live by Him."

1 John 5:6

"This is He that came by water and blood, Jesus Christ: not by water only, but by water and blood. And it is the Spirit which testifieth, that Christ is the TRUTH."

1 John 5:20

"And we know that the Son of God is come: and He hath given us understanding that we may know the TRUE GOD, and may be in HIS TRUE SON."

p. Titus 2:11-13

"For the grace of God our Saviour hath appeared to all men; instructing us. ... Looking for the blessed hope and coming of the glory of the great God and our Saviour Jesus Christ."

BOOK THREE

God Sent His Own Beloved Son

BASAL MATERIAL

FOR

DISCUSSING OR TEACHING

BOOK THREE:

GOD SENT HIS OWN BELOVED SON

79

Book Three:

God Sent His Own Beloved Son

A. INTRODUCTORY

A Scientific Plan for Presenting Doctrinal Truths

It is poor psychology to give new information to a child without first exploring the background of knowledge he already possesses which would have an association with the new truth about to be taught. For each one of us assimilates new knowledge in the light of old knowledge already accumulated. Consequently, good interpretation of a new doctrine being taught depends to a large extent upon the thoroughness of the apperceptive basis. And this is the reason why careful exploration and the laying of a good apperceptive basis is so very necessary.

It might be of interest to note how frequently Jesus, the Wisest of Teachers, applies this principle in His teaching.

In the series "A LITTLE CHILD'S FIRST COMMUNION" this psychological principle has been carefully heeded in the teaching of each doctrine, and each book forms an apperceptive basis for the book which follows.

For example: in Book Two, "God's Own Son" was INTRODUCED to the child as:

THE GOD-MAN;

THE GREATEST AND HOLIEST TEACHER THE WORLD COULD EVER HAVE;

THE ONE WHO HAD THE POWER TO OFFER TO HIS FATHER SUCH GREAT LOVE AND OBEDIENCE THAT HE WOULD MORE THAN MAKE UP FOR THE TURNING AWAY FROM GOD OF OUR FIRST PARENTS AND ALL THOSE WHO WOULD COME AFTER THEM;

and

THE ONE THROUGH WHOSE POWER GOD'S LOVE AND TRUTH (SANCTIFYING GRACE) WOULD BE GIVEN TO THE PEOPLE.

81

And this teaching given in Book Two forms an apperceptive basis for the teaching in Books Three and Four concerning the doctrines of THE INCARNATION, THE REDEMPTION and THE FOUNDING OF JESUS' CHURCH. For in Books Three and Four STORIES CONCERNING THE BIRTH, LIFE AND DEATH OF JESUS are told in clear, childlike language, and are so motivated that these fundamental doctrines stand out in bold relief.

In the process of teaching a new doctrine, when the apperceptive basis has been carefully laid, something should be said, or some questions asked, which would arouse in the child curiosity concerning the new knowledge about to be presented. In other words, before the new knowledge is presented, there should be some MOTIVATION, or CHALLENGE, which would cause the child to be interested in receiving it.

From a study of the Gospels we see that Jesus, when teaching, made use of the principle of motivation. Some instances are the Parables, the Last Judgment (Matthew 25:32-46) and the Samaritan woman at Jacob's Well (John 4:5-27).

After the motivation, the new knowledge should be presented in a way that will cause the greatest amount of self-activity on the part of the child. In the Parable of the Talents, Jesus emphasizes the principle of self-activity (Matthew 25:14-29).

After the new knowledge has been presented in this way, it should then be organized into the condensed theological statements which were the teacher's objective and to which he intended, from the beginning, to lead the child.

This way of leading the child gradually, step by step, through a drawing-out process, to think out the theological statement for himself before discovering it in the catechism, is called THE INDUCTIVE PROCESS.

But when the meaning of the theological statement or point of doctrine has been assimilated by the child, he must then learn, through related activities, TO APPLY the principle. No good teacher will consider a lesson finished until the number of applications carried out indicates a mastery of the principle. This part of the lesson is A DEDUCTIVE PROCESS.

In general a due respect for the child-mind and an understanding of it mean that teachers will not force applications upon the child before he has thoroughly grasped the doctrine being taught.

For when zealous but not understanding teachers force applications which have proceeded from their own assimilation of the principle, but not from the child's, the result is a great distaste for doctrine.

After the child has been taught in simple language, in Book Three, the main facts in the Life of Jesus, AS AN APPLICATION there is a section entitled "Stories Telling How to Be Like Jesus."

Keeping in mind that this series aims to form the child's conscience in preparation for a first Confession, THE VIRTUES WHICH ARE IN OPPOSITION TO VIOLATIONS OF THE COMMANDMENTS OF GOD should first be presented to the child. And these virtues should be presented as exemplified in the Life of Jesus. For the child should be taught always to look to Jesus as OUR MODEL. This is very important, and in departing from it there is danger, when the child is very young, of exaggerated and unsound ideas of virtue.

This incident, which was told me by a superintendent of schools, will make my meaning clearer. A prominent man who was asked to speak to a large group of boys in a State School urged them to choose a hero and to study and copy this hero. He then gave a short sketch of the lives of some great men whom they might look up to as heroes, among them Benjamin Franklin. The next day, bright and early, seven of the boys had packed their bags and started out for Philadelphia.

Jesus is the truest Model for each stage of our lives, and this is the wisest and best teaching to be given to the child in these beginning lessons.

Since the teacher should have in mind that these stories are given as a foundation upon which to build the examination of conscience, considerable time should be given to their assimilation; simple project work would be an aid to assimilation, to interest and to a deeper understanding of the virtues.

As a fitting close to the study of the Life of Jesus, and as a helpful motivation for a substantial examination of conscience and a good Confession, Jesus' TWO GREAT COMMANDMENTS OF LOVE are carefully presented.

B. DOCTRINAL TRUTHS PRESENTED TO THE CHILD IN BOOK THREE WITH THE EXPECTATION THAT HE WILL UNDERSTAND AND APPRECIATE THEM IN ACCORDANCE WITH HIS MENTAL AGE:

That:

1. to restore the Order of Justice after sin had been committed required Someone Who had greater power to love, to obey and to suffer than any creature had;

2. Jesus is the true Son of God;

3. Jesus offered to His Father more than enough love and obedience and suffering to make up for the turning away from God of our first parents, and of all His brethren from the beginning to the end of the world;

4. Jesus is Truth come to earth;

5. Jesus taught Truth and did everything with Love;

6. all doctrine concerning the Godhead and right living must be based upon Jesus' teachings;

7. Jesus gave two commandments upon which to base our progress in the spiritual life;

8. Mary was the Immaculate Conception, since it is taught on page 3 that "from the very beginning of her life, Mary was filled with God's Love and Truth";

9. Mary was chosen by God to be the Mother of His Own Son;

10. St. Joseph was not the father of Jesus; God was Jesus' Father;

11. Mary was a virgin mother; St. Joseph was chosen by God to be the protector of Jesus and Mary;

12. St. Joseph, the Magi and the shepherds had great faith;

13. the Holy Ghost Who dwells within souls bright with the Light of Grace is ever teaching them and ever sanctifying them by pouring into the very depths of their being Divine Love and Truth;

14. in God there are Three Persons: the Father, the Son and the Holy Ghost;

15. we call the Three Persons in One God the Holy Trinity.

C. GROWTH IN POWER TO BE EXPECTED IN THE CHILD AS A RESULT OF STUDYING BOOK THREE:

Greater facility:

1. in understanding the Life of Jesus and the principles He taught;

2. in combating what is against Christ and His principles;

3. in studying ways of being more like Jesus;

4. in prayer and in expressing love for God;

5. in meditating upon the life of the Blessed Virgin and in striving to imitate her purity;

6. in striving for an increase of grace and in listening to the inspirations of the Holy Ghost;

7. in making a Catechism Project Book.

D. PEDAGOGICAL STRUCTURE

In all proceedings, whether in the realm of organization or teaching, when these proceedings are moving smoothly and happily, we know that there has been a well-laid plan.

In order to bring about religious teaching which is permeated with both interest and joy, a well-laid scientific plan for presenting a doctrinal truth is also necessary.

But if in our religious teaching we can associate both interest and joy with each doctrine taught, we shall be doing much for the spread of religion.

For interest and joy are contagious.

The following outline will help to bring about this ideal in our teaching of the doctrinal truths of Book Three.

Teacher's Major Objective

Through teaching and meditation on the Life of Jesus to develop in the child-mind a positive personal love of Jesus together with a desire to follow Him as Model; to develop a realization of the Personality of the Holy Ghost; and to impart the idea that in the One True God there are three separate Persons.

Exploration and Establishment of an Apperceptive Background for the New Knowledge

This part of the lesson is an exploration into the child's mind to discover what he already knows which would dovetail into the new subject-matter about to be presented and establish an appropriate apperceptive background for it.

a. Pertinent questions by the teacher relating to the Godhead as taught in Books One and Two;

b. Pertinent questions by the teacher concerning the failure of our first parents to give God love and obedience; God's Merciful Promise; the Prophets (Book Two);

c. Pertinent questions by the teacher relating to the coming of God's Own Son as taught in Book Two.

Motivation

a. For the child — see Introductory page

b. For the teacher:
The Order of Justice had been upset by the sin of Adam. In the Mind of God there was a wonderful plan which would restore the Order of Justice.

Presentation of New Knowledge

Generalizations

a. God wanted His Own Beloved Son to become one of us so that He could do for us what no one else could do, that is to redeem all people and to leave a Sure Way, "a Holy Way, a Straight Way," so that all people could have and keep His Love and Truth in them.

b. Jesus, God's Own Beloved Son, lived upon this earth and suffered and died to give to His Father so much love and obedience that He more than made up for the failure in love and obedience of Adam and all the other people belonging to Adam's family from the beginning to the end of the world.
(The second part of Jesus' Mission will be taught in Book Four.)

c. Jesus sent the Holy Ghost to keep on teaching God's Truth until the end of the world and to sanctify us by "pouring forth into our hearts" God's Love and Truth.

d. In One God there are Three Persons, the Father, the Son and the Holy Ghost. We call the Three Persons in One God the Holy Trinity.

Applications and Related Activities

E. THEOLOGICAL BACKGROUND

As one reads excerpts from the Doctors of the Church and realizes the scholarly searching and stately unfolding of each doctrine, there arise an interest and joy both pure and delightful. And when this study is continuous, day by day, the interest and joy become permanent and are bound to lift one to a higher plane of living.

Anyone who studies the excerpts given in this section must necessarily experience enlightenment and a taste of the pure joy which comes from a searching study of doctrine such as is given by these Doctors of the Church.

1. The Immaculate Conception

a. Definition of the Immaculate Conception of the Blessed Virgin Mary (given by Pope Pius IX, December 8, 1854).
"For the honor of the Holy and Undivided Trinity, for the glory and adornment of the Virgin Mother of God, for the exaltation of the Catholic faith and the increase of the Christian religion, We declare, pronounce and define, by the authority of our Lord Jesus Christ, of the blessed Apostles Peter and Paul, and Our own, that the doctrine which holds that the most Blessed Virgin Mary, in the first instant of her conception, was, by the singular grace and privilege of God, in view of the merits of Jesus Christ, the Saviour of the human race, preserved free from every stain of original sin, has been revealed by God and is therefore to be firmly and constantly believed by all the faithful. Wherefore if any should presume, which God forbid, to think otherwise in their hearts than We have defined, let them know and be certain that they have been condemned by their own judgment, that they have made shipwreck in faith, that they have fallen away from the unity of the Church; and furthermore, that, should they dare to manifest in word and writing, or in any other external way, what they think in their hearts, they subject themselves by this very act to the penalties prescribed by the law."
Catechism of the Council of Trent, Appendix I.

2. Mary, Like All Other Human Beings, Had Free Will

a. "It was reasonable that it should be announced to the Blessed Virgin that she was to conceive Christ . . . that she might offer to God the free gift of her obedience: which she proved herself right ready to do, saying: 'Behold the handmaid of the Lord.' "
St. Thomas Aquinas, "Summa Theologica,"
Part Three, Second Number, Q. XXX, Art. I.

3. Christ Was Conceived by the Holy Ghost in the Womb of the Virgin Mary

a. "Just as it was possible for the first man to be produced, by the Divine power, from the slime of the earth, so too it was possible for Christ's body to be made, by Divine power, from a virgin without the seed of the male."

Ibid., Q. XXVIII, Art. I.

b. "What means this closed gate in the House of the Lord, except that Mary is to be ever inviolate? . . . And what is this — 'The Lord alone enters in and goeth out by it' — except that the Holy Ghost shall impregnate her, and that the Lord of angels shall be born of her? And what means this — 'It shall be shut for evermore' — but that Mary is a Virgin before His Birth, a Virgin in His Birth, and a Virgin after His Birth?"

St. Augustine, "De Annunt. Dom.," III on Ezechiel XLIV, 2.

c. "The temporal nativity by which Christ was born for our salvation is, in a way, natural, since a Man was born of a woman, and after the due lapse of time from His conception; but it is also supernatural, because He was begotten, not of seed, but of the Holy Ghost and the Blessed Virgin, above the law of conception."

St. John Damascene, "De Fide Orthod.," III.

d. "We must say that the Blessed Virgin is called the Mother of God, not as though she were the Mother of the Godhead, but because she is the Mother, according to His human nature, of the Person Who has both the Divine and the human nature."

St. Thomas Aquinas, loc. cit., Q. XXXV, Art. 4.

e. "Neither did she 'multiply her conception' nor was she 'under man's' — her husband's — power (Genesis III:16), who in her spotless womb conceived Christ of the Holy Ghost."

St. Augustine, "De Assump. B. V. M."

f. "The expression 'of whom was born Jesus' signifies that the Virgin was the real Mother of Jesus, i. e., of that Man Who, being hypostatically united with God, was both God and Man. Therefore was she truly the Mother of God. For although she was not the Mother of Deity, yet did she give birth to God, because she was the Mother of that Man. For that Man was God, therefore the Blessed Virgin was Mother of God. . . . The Person of the Son of God, Who is God, is rightly spoken of as born of the Virgin Mary, but according to His human, not His Divine nature."

Cornelius à Lapide (St. Matthew 1:16).

g. "The expression 'of whom was born' signifies that the Holy Ghost was the most potent and efficient cause of the Nativity of Christ, Who, within the Blessed Virgin, of her most pure blood, formed the Body of Christ, organized It and gave It life, and hypostatically united It to the Word in the first moment of Its conception."

Ibid.

h. "The whole Trinity effected the conception of Christ's body: nevertheless this is attributed to the Holy Ghost."

St. Thomas Aquinas, loc. cit., Q. XXXII, Art. I.

i. "This conception had three privileges — namely, that it was without original sin, that it was not that of a man only, but of God and Man, and that it was a virginal conception. And all three were effected by the Holy Ghost."

Ibid., Art. IV.

4. The Mother of Christ Was a Virgin

a. "To the substance of a body in which was the Godhead, closed doors were no obstacle. For truly He had power to enter in by doors not open, in Whose birth His Mother's virginity remained inviolate."

St. Augustine, "Sup. Joan.," Tract. 121.

b. "We must confess simply that the Mother of Christ was a Virgin in conceiving: for to deny this belongs to the heresy of the Ebionites and Cerinthus, who held Christ to be a mere man, and maintained that He was born of both sexes."

St. Thomas Aquinas, loc. cit., Q. XXVIII, Art. I.

c. "Without any hesitation, we must abhor the error of Helvidius, who dared to assert that Christ's Mother, after His birth, was carnally known by Joseph, and bore other children."

Ibid., Art. III.

d. "The Mother of God is called [Joseph's] wife from the first promise of her espousals, whom he had not known nor ever was to know by carnal intercourse."

St. Augustine, "De Nup. et Concep.," I.

5. St. Joseph

a. "The ministry and office of Joseph was most noble, in that it pertains to the order of the hypostatic union of the Word with our flesh. For Joseph exercised all his labors and actions in immediate proximity to the Person of Christ."

Cornelius à Lapide (St. Matthew 1:16).

b. Though Joseph was not the father of our Lord and Saviour, the order of His genealogy is traced down to Joseph. . . . The Scriptures are not wont to trace the female line in genealogies: secondly, Mary and Joseph were of the same tribe."

St. Jerome on Matthew 1:18.

c. "It was befitting to trace that genealogy down to Joseph . . . for truth suffered nothing thereby, since both Joseph and Mary were of the family of David."

St. Augustine, loc. cit.

d. "Christ willed to be born in Bethlehem . . . because . . . 'He was made . . . of the seed of David according to the flesh,' . . . as it is written [Romans 1:3]. . . . He willed to be born at Bethlehem, where David was born, in order that by the very birthplace the promise made to David might be shown to be fulfilled."

St. Thomas Aquinas, loc. cit., Q. XXXV, Art. VII.

6. The Blessed Virgin Mary Was Always Full of Grace

a. "We must therefore confess simply that the Blessed Virgin committed no actual sin, neither mortal nor venial: so that what is written [Canticle 4:7] is fulfilled: 'Thou art all fair, O my love, and there is not a spot in thee.' "

Ibid., Q. XXVII, Art. IV.

7. The Blessed Virgin Mary Knew the Prophecies
Concerning the Expected Messias

a. "The Blessed Virgin did indeed believe explicitly in the future Incarnation; but being humble, she did not think such high things of herself. Consequently she required instruction in this matter."

Ibid., Q. XXX, Art. I.

8. Mary Was the Second Eve

a. "Mary the Virgin is found obedient, saying, 'Behold the handmaid of the Lord; be it done unto me according to Thy word.' But Eve was disobedient, ... having become disobedient, was made the cause of death both to herself and to the entire human race; so also did Mary, ... by yielding obedience, become the cause of salvation both to herself and the whole human race. ... The knot of Eve's disobedience was loosed by the obedience of Mary. For what the virgin Eve bound fast through unbelief, this did the Virgin Mary set free through faith."

*St. Irenaeus, "Adv. Haer.," III:22-24.

b. "It was while Eve was yet a virgin that the ensnaring word had crept into her ear which was to build the edifice of death. Into a virgin's soul in like manner must be introduced the Word of God which was to raise the fabric of life: so that what had been reduced to ruin by this sex might by the selfsame sex be recovered to salvation."

*Tertullian, "On the Flesh of Christ," C. XVII.

c. "If death came through woman, life came through the Blessed Virgin. ... Therefore if evil came from woman, so does good; for if we have fallen in Eve, we stand in Mary. We were given up to slavery through Eve and are made free through Mary. ... Eve caused our condemnation through the apple of the tree. Mary wiped it out through the mystery of the tree because Christ hung on it as its fruit. ... We are borne down to earth through Eve and are raised to heaven through Mary."

*St. Augustine, "Nova Pat. Bibliotheca," tom. 1, p. 1.

d. "Great and exceeding wrong, my most dearly beloved, has been done to us by one man and one woman; but thanks be to God, by One Man and one Woman ... great have been the graces given to us by God out of the old Adam to form for us a new Adam and to transform Eve into Mary."

*St. Bernard, "Sermon on the Prerogatives of the Blessed Virgin."

e. "Behold, O man, the counsel of God, the counsel of Wisdom, the counsel of Love. ... He Who was about to redeem the human race, brought with Him into Mary and bestowed upon her the whole ransom. Why was this? Haply that excuse might be made for Eve through her daughter, and that the complaint of the man against the woman might henceforth be hushed to sleep forever."

*St. Bernard, "De Aquaed.," VI.

* Acknowledgment, with appreciation, is given to Burns, Oates & Washbourne, London, for permission to quote these passages from Chapters III and IV of *The Greater Eve*.

9. Angels

a. "There is a threefold truth, in heart, word and deed. The truth of the heart is opposed to error; the truth of word is opposed to a lie, the truth of deed is when a man acts in accordance with what is practically right, and this is opposed to iniquity and sin. Now the devil did not stand in the truth because he did not persevere in what he ought to have done. He refused to be under God. He claimed to be His equal, a kind of second god, and rose up against Him through pride. Hence he fell from his state of grace and was cast down to hell (see Isaias 14:12)."

Cornelius à Lapide (St. John 8:44).

b. "Bede says in a homily on the Annunciation: 'It was an apt beginning of man's restoration that an angel should be sent by God to the Virgin who was to be hallowed by the Divine birth; since the first cause of man's ruin was through the serpent being sent by the devil to cajole the woman by the spirit of pride.' "

St. Thomas Aquinas, loc. cit., Q. XXX, Art. II.

c. "Gabriel means 'Power of God.' The message therefore was fittingly brought by the 'Power of God,' because the Lord of hosts and mighty in battle was coming to overcome the powers of the air."

St. Gregory, "De Centum Ovibus."

10. Jesus Was the Son of God; He Was Also the Son of the Virgin Mary. Therefore He Was God and Man — He Was All-Holy

a. "In the first instant of conception, Christ's body was both animated and assumed by the Word. Consequently, in the first instant of His conception, Christ had the fulness of grace sanctifying His body and His soul. But the mystery of the Incarnation is considered as a condescension of the fulness of the Godhead into human nature...."

St. Thomas Aquinas, loc. cit., Q. XXXIV, Art. I.

b. "Pope Leo says ... Christ's soul excels our soul not by diversity of genus, but by solemnity of power; for it is of the same genus as our souls, yet excels even the angels in FULNESS OF GRACE AND TRUTH."

Ibid., First Number, Q. VI, Art. III.

c. "As soon as the Word entered the womb, while retaining the reality of His Nature, He was made flesh and a perfect man."

St. Gregory, "Regist.," XI, quoting St. Augustine.

d. "But Christ, in the first instant of His conception, had the fulness of sanctifying grace, and in like manner the fulness of known truth; according to John 1:14 'full of grace and truth.' "

St. Thomas Aquinas, loc. cit.,
Second Number, Q. XXXIV, Art. II.

e. "Since Christ was both God and man, He had, even in His humanity, something more than other creatures — namely that He was in the state of beatitude from the very beginning."

Ibid., Art. IV.

f. "But because for us and for our salvation, uniting the human nature to His Person, He became the child of a woman, for this reason do we say that He was born in the flesh" (St. Cyril).

Ibid., Q. XXXV, Art. II.

g. "To show that He is of the same nature as the Father, He is called the Son; to show that He is co-eternal, He is called the Splendor; to show that He is altogether like, He is called the Image; to show that He is begotten immaterially, He is called the Word. All these truths cannot be expressed by only one Name."

Ibid., Part One, Second Number, Q. XXXIV, Art. II.

h. "For, as Pope Leo says in a sermon on the Epiphany (Chrysostom, 'Hom. II in Matth.') :
" 'Herod was not so much troubled in himself as the devil in Herod. For Herod thought Him to be a man, but the devil thought Him to be God. Each feared a successor to his kingdom: the devil, a heavenly successor; Herod, an earthly successor.' But their fear was needless: since Christ had not come to set up an earthly kingdom, as Pope Leo says, addressing himself to Herod: 'Thy palace cannot hold Christ: nor is the Lord of the world content with the paltry power of thy sceptre.' "

Ibid., Part Three, Second Number, Q. XXXVI, Art. II.

i. "The shepherds were Israelites, the Magi were Gentiles. The former were nigh to Him, the latter far from Him. Both hastened to Him together as to the corner-stone."

St. Augustine, "Sermon on the Epiphany," C. C. T.

j. "It was not without reason that Christ's birth was made known by means of angels to the shepherds, who, being Jews, were accustomed to frequent apparitions of the angels; whereas it was revealed by means of a star to the Magi, who were wont to consider the heavenly bodies."

St. Thomas Aquinas, loc. cit., Art. V.

k. "Or we may say, as may be read in the book 'De Qq. Nov. et Vet. Test.,' LXIII, that 'these Magi followed the tradition of Balaam, who said, "A star shall rise out of Jacob." Wherefore observing this star to be a stranger to the system of this world, they gathered that it was the one foretold by Balaam to indicate the King of the Jews.' "

Ibid.

l. "By proclaiming [Christ King] the Magi foreshadowed the constancy of the Gentiles in confessing Christ even until death."

Ibid., Art. VII.

m. "Since, therefore, this prerogative of grace was bestowed on the Man Christ that through Him all men might be saved, therefore He was becomingly named Jesus, i. e., Saviour. . . . When it was said, 'His name shall be called Wonderful . . . the Prince of Peace,' the way and term of our salvation are pointed out; inasmuch as ' by the wonderful counsel and might of the Godhead we are brought to the inheritance of the life to come,' in which the children of God will enjoy *'perfect peace'* under 'God their Prince.' "

Ibid., Q. XXXVII, Art. II.

n. "Christ wished to make His Godhead known through His human nature. And therefore, since it is proper to man to do so, He associated with men, at the same time manifesting His Godhead to all by preaching and working miracles, and by leading among men a blameless and righteous life."

Ibid., Q. XL, Art. I.

o. "Christ conformed His conduct in all things to the precepts of the Law."

Ibid., Q. XL, Art. IV.

p. "By men a thing can be recalled to the mind by the use of word-signs but it is the incorruptible Truth itself that teaches, the one true, the sole interior Master. He became an exterior Teacher also, that He might recall us from exterior to interior things, and taking the form of a servant, He deigned to appear in lowliness to the lowly, that His sublimity might become clear to those rising up to Him."

St. Augustine, "Contra ep. fund.," XXXVI, 41.

11.   Jesus Came to Redeem the World

a. "Now Christ came into the world and taught in order to save man, according to John 3:17. . . . Therefore it was fitting that Christ by miraculously healing men in particular should prove Himself to be the Universal and Spiritual Saviour of all."

St. Thomas Aquinas, loc. cit., Q. XLIV, Art. III.

b. "Christ was called a Lamb by Isaias and Jeremias, Who was to be offered for the redemption of the world. He is called a Lamb because of His lamblike innocence, meekness, patience and obedience, even unto death, which like a lamb, He bore in silence. As St. Peter says, 'Who when He was reviled, reviled not again: when He suffered, He threatened not; but committed Himself to Him that judgeth righteously' (1 Peter 2:23)."

Cornelius à Lapide (St. John 1:29).

c. "Who taketh away the sin: taketh away, both as regards the stain which sin in act imprints upon the soul, and as regards the guilt of sin which makes the sinner liable to hell. This He takes away by making expiation, and bearing the punishment in Himself; thus is justice and equity satisfying for sin by His death upon the cross. . . . God made Him the victim for the sins of the whole world, that He might sanctify all who repent and believe in Him."

Ibid.

d. "That man should be delivered by Christ's Passion was in keeping with both His mercy and His justice. With His justice, because by His Passion Christ made satisfaction for the sin of the human race, and so man was set free by Christ's justice; and with His mercy, for since man of himself could not satisfy for the sin of all human nature, . . . God gave him His Son to satisfy for him, according to Romans 3:24, 25."

St. Thomas Aquinas, loc. cit., Q. XLVI, Art. I.

e. "Man was delivered by Christ's Passion. Many other things besides deliverance from sin concurred for man's salvation. In the first place man knows thereby how much God loves him, and is thereby stirred to love Him in return, and herein lies the perfection of human salvation; hence the Apostle says [Romans 5:8]. . . . Secondly, because thereby He set us an example of obedience, humility, constancy, justice, and the other virtues displayed in the Passion which are requisite for man's salvation. Hence it is written [1 Peter 2:21]. Thirdly, because Christ by His Passion not only delivered man from sin, but also merited justifying grace for him and the glory of bliss. . . . Fourthly, because man is all the more bound to refrain from sin, when he bears in mind that he has been redeemed by Christ's Blood, according to 1 Corinthians 6:20. Fifthly, because it redounded to man's greater dignity, that as man was overcome and deceived by the devil, so also it should be a Man that should overthrow the devil; and as man deserved death so a Man by dying should vanquish death. Hence it is written [1 Corinthians 15:57]. . . .

"Although the devil assailed man unjustly, nevertheless, on account of sin, man was justly left by God under the devil's bondage. And therefore it was fitting that through justice man should be delivered from the devil's bondage by Christ making satisfaction on his behalf in the Passion. This was also a fitting means of overthrowing the pride of the devil 'who is a deserter from justice, and covetous of sway,' in that Christ 'should vanquish him and deliver man, not merely by the power of His Godhead, but likewise by the justice and lowliness of the Passion,' as Augustine says ('De Trin.,' XIII)."

Ibid., Art. III.

f. "Two thieves are set, one upon His right and one upon His left, to show that all mankind is called to the sacrament of His Passion. But because of the cleavage between believers and unbelievers, the multitude is divided into right and left, those on the right side being saved by the justification of faith."

St. Hilary, "Cap. XXX in Matth."

g. "He properly atones for an offense who offers something which the offended one loves equally, or even more than he detested the offense. But by suffering out of love and obedience, Christ gave more to God than was required to compensate for the offense of the whole human race. . . . Christ's love was greater than His slayers' malice, and therefore the value of His Passion in atoning surpassed the murderous guilt of those who crucified Him: so much so that Christ's suffering was sufficient and superabundant atonement for His murderers' crime."

St. Thomas Aquinas, loc. cit., Q. XLVIII, Art. II.

h. "It was fitting for Christ to die. First of all to satisfy for the whole human race, which was sentenced to die on account of sin (Genesis 2:17). . . . Now it is a fitting way of satisfying for another to submit oneself to the penalty deserved by that other. And so Christ resolved to die, that by dying He might atone for us (1 Peter 3:18)."

Ibid., Q. L, Art. I.

12. Christ the Head of the Mystical Body

a. "Grace was bestowed upon Christ, not only as an individual but inasmuch as He is the Head of the Church, so that it might overflow into His members; and therefore Christ's works are referred to Himself and to His members in the same way as the works of any other man in a state of grace are referred to himself. But it is evident that whosoever suffers for justice' sake, provided that he be in a state of grace, merits his salvation thereby, according to Matthew 5:10. Consequently Christ by His Passion merited salvation, not only for Himself, but likewise for all His members."

Ibid., Q. XLVIII, Art. I.

b. "Christ's satisfaction works its effect in us inasmuch as we are incorporated with Him, as the members with their head. . . . Now the members must be conformed with their head. Consequently, as Christ first had grace in His soul with bodily passibility, and through the Passion attained to the glory of immortality, so we likewise, who are His members, are freed by His Passion from all debt of punishment, yet so that we receive in our souls 'the spirit of adoption of sons,' whereby our names are written down for the inheritance of immortal glory, while we yet have a passible and mortal body; but afterward, 'being made conformable' to the sufferings and death of Christ, we are brought into immortal glory, according to the saying of the Apostle [Romans 8:17]."

Ibid., Q. XLIX, Art. 3.

13. The Resurrection and Ascension

a. "What tidings could we call as good as that our Saviour rose from the dead; and what greater thing could they preach than that which the women made known to them? But why did woman announce the evangel? Because through a woman death was amended. For the woman giving tidings of life consoled the woman giving tidings of death, since she was dead, giving the cup of death. By the woman was Adam seduced, so that he fell into death, by woman was Christ proclaimed as being risen and never more to die."

St. Augustine, "Ser. XLV," 5.

b. "It behooved Christ to rise again. . . . First of all, for the commendation of Divine Justice, to which it belongs to exalt them who humble themselves for God's sake, according to Luke 1:52. . . . Consequently, because Christ humbled Himself even to the death of the Cross from love and obedience to God, it behooved Him to be uplifted by God to a glorious resurrection; . . . secondly, for our instruction in the faith, since our belief in Christ's Godhead is confirmed by His rising again; . . . thirdly, for the raising of our hope, since through seeing Christ Who is our head rise again, we hope that we likewise shall rise again. . . ."

St. Thomas Aquinas, loc. cit., Q. LIII, Art. I.

c. "There is a twofold nature in Christ, to wit, the Divine and the human. Hence His own power can be accepted according to both. Likewise a twofold power can be accepted regarding His human nature. One is natural, flowing from the principles of nature; and it is quite evident that Christ did not ascend into heaven by such power as this. The other is the power of glory, which is in Christ's human nature; and it was according to this that He ascended into heaven."

Ibid., Q. LVII, Art. III.

14. The Holy Trinity

a. "It is proper to Christ as man to be the Redeemer immediately; although the Redemption may be ascribed to the whole Trinity as its first cause."

Ibid., Q. XLVIII, Art. V.

b. "Because the Holy Ghost is common to both, He Himself is called that properly which both are called in common. For the Father also is a Spirit, and the Son is a Spirit; and the Father is holy, and the Son is holy."

St. Augustine, "De Trin.," XV.

c. "For the reason that the Holy Ghost proceeds from the Father perfectly, not only is it not superfluous to say He proceeds from the Son, but rather it is absolutely necessary. For as much as one power belongs to the Father and the Son; and whatever is from the Father must be from the Son, unless it is opposed to the property of Filiation; for the Son is not from Himself, although He is from the Father. The Holy Ghost is distinguished personally from the Son, inasmuch as the origin of the one is distinguished from the origin of the other; but the difference itself of origin comes from the fact that the Son is only from the Father, whereas the Holy Ghost is from the Father and the Son."

St. Thomas Aquinas, op. cit.,
Part I, Second Number, Q. XXXVI, Art. II.

d. "As the Son is properly called the Image because He proceeds by way of the Word, Whose nature it is to be the similitude of its principle, although the Holy Ghost also is like to the Father; so also, because the Holy Ghost proceeds from the Father as Love, He is properly called Gift, although the Son, too, is given. For that the Son is given is from the Father's Love, according to the words [John 3:16]."

Ibid., Q. XXXVIII, Art. II.

e. "In the Trinity, the Holy Ghost, the sweetness of the Begetter and the Begotten, pours out upon us His bounty and richness."

St. Augustine, "De Trin.," VI.

f. "The Holy Ghost is the sign that the Father loves the Son inasmuch as the Holy Ghost proceeds from them both as Love."

St. Thomas Aquinas, loc. cit., Q. XXXVII, Art. II.

g. "Keep me, I pray, in this expression of my faith, that I may ever possess the Father — namely Thyself; that I may adore Thy Son together with Thee; and that I may deserve Thy Holy Spirit, Who is through Thy Only-Begotten."

St. Hilary, "De Trin.," XII.

h. The Athanasian Creed says:

The Father is Uncreated;

The Son is Uncreated;

The Holy Ghost is Uncreated;
    And yet there are not three uncreated beings,
    but one Uncreated Being.

The Father is Eternal;

The Son is Eternal;

The Holy Ghost is Eternal;
    And yet there are not three eternals, but one Eternal.

The Father is Infinite;

The Son is Infinite;

The Holy Ghost is Infinite;
    And yet there are not three infinites, but one Infinite.

The Father is Almighty;

The Son is Almighty;

The Holy Ghost is Almighty;
    And yet there are not three almighties, but one Almighty.

The Father is God;

The Son is God;

The Holy Ghost is God;
    And yet there are not three gods, but only one God.

15. Prayer

a. "Prayer occupied the entire life of Jesus; for what else was His sojourn upon earth than an unspeakably holy and mysterious life of prayer, intercession, meditation and contemplation? He prayed in the crib. . . . During His public life He frequently retired to secluded places, chiefly to mountains, there to pray and to watch throughout the night in prayer; praying He raised His eyes to heaven before working miracles or imparting blessings; . . . the whole time of His Passion. . . . He continued to offer most humble, fervent, sacrificial prayer."

*Gihr, "The Holy Sacrifice of the Mass," p. 74.

* Acknowledgment, with appreciation, is given to B. Herder and Company, St. Louis, Missouri, for permission to quote passages from Gihr, *The Holy Sacrifice of the Mass,* here and on pages 141-156 and 204.

16. The Our Father

a. "The Lord's Prayer is most perfect because, as Augustine says to Proba ('Epist.,' CXXX), if we pray rightly and fittingly we can say nothing else but what is contained in this prayer of our Lord. . . . In the Lord's Prayer not only do we ask for all that we may rightly desire, but also in the order wherein we ought to desire them; so that this prayer not only teaches us to ask, but also directs all our affections. Thus it is evident that the first thing to be the object of our desire is the end, and afterward whatever is directed to the end. Now our end is God, toward Whom our affections tend in two ways; first, by our willing the glory of God, secondly, by willing to enjoy His glory. The first belongs to the love whereby we love God in Himself, while the second belongs to the love whereby we love ourselves in God. Wherefore the first petition is expressed thus: 'Hallowed be Thy name,' and the second thus: 'Thy kingdom come,' by which we ask to come to the glory of His kingdom."

St. Thomas Aquinas, op. cit.,
Part II, Second Part, Q. LXXXIII, Art. IX.

b. " 'Thus therefore ye shall pray: Our Father,' etc. Christ here delivers to Christians a method of prayer, but He does not command that we should use these words and none else, but only teaches the things which should be asked of God, and in what order and with what brevity they may be asked. Well, however, does the Church use these very words of Christ, as being divine, most brief, clear and efficacious. Whence St. Cyprian ('Trac. de Orat. Domini') says: 'What can be more real prayer to the Father than that which proceeded from the mouth of the Son, Who is the Truth?' "

Cornelius à Lapide (St. Matthew 6:9).

17. The Commandments of the Old and the New Law

a. "The Old Law contained some moral precepts; as is evident from Exodus 20:13, 15. This was reasonable: because, just as the principal intention of human law is to create friendship between man and man; so this chief intention of the Divine Law is to establish man in friendship with God. Now since likeness is the reason of love, according to Ecclesiasticus 13:19, there cannot possibly be any friendship of man to God, Who is supremely good, unless man become good: wherefore it is written (Leviticus 19:2), 'You shall be holy, for I am holy.' But the goodness of man is virtue, which makes its subject good ('Ethic.,' II). Therefore it was necessary for the Old Law to include precepts about acts of virtue; and these are the moral precepts of the Law."

St. Thomas Aquinas, loc. cit.,
First Part, Third Number, Q. XCIX, Art. II.

b. "The precepts of the Decalogue differ from the other precepts of the Law, in the fact that God Himself is said to have given the precepts of the Decalogue; whereas He gave the other precepts to the people through Moses. Wherefore the Decalogue includes those precepts the knowledge of which man has immediately from God."

Ibid., Q. C, Art. III.

c. "The same God gave both the New and the Old Law, but in different ways. For He gave the Old Law written on tables of stone: whereas He gave the New Law written in the fleshly tables of the heart, as the Apostle expresses it (2 Corinthians 3:3)."

Ibid., Q. CVI, Art. II.

d. " ... The state of the New Law succeeded the state of the Old Law, as a more perfect law a less perfect one. Now no state of the present life can be more perfect than the state of the New Law: since nothing can approach nearer to the last end than that which is the immediate cause of our being brought to the last end. But the New Law does this. ... "

Ibid., CVI, Art. IV.

e. "All the differences assigned between the Old and New Laws are gathered from their relative perfection and imperfection. For the precepts of every law prescribe acts of virtue. Now the imperfect, who as yet are not possessed of a virtuous habit, are directed in one way to perform virtuous acts, while those who are perfected by the possession of virtuous habits are directed in another way. For those who as yet are not endowed with virtuous habits are directed to the performance of virtuous acts by reason of some outward cause: for instance, by the threat of punishment, or the promise of some extrinsic reward, such as honor, riches, or the like. Hence the Old Law, which was given to men who were imperfect, that is, who had not yet received spiritual grace, was called the *law of fear,* inasmuch as it induced men to observe its commandments by threatening them with penalties; and is spoken of as containing temporal promises. On the other hand, those who are possessed of virtue are inclined to do virtuous deeds through love of virtue, not on account of some extrinsic punishment or reward. Hence the New Law, which derives its preëminence from the spiritual grace instilled into our hearts, is called the *law of love:* and it is described as containing spiritual and eternal promises, which are objects of the virtues, chiefly charity. Accordingly, such persons are inclined of themselves to those objects, not as to something foreign but as to something of their own. For this reason, too, the Old Law is described as restraining the hand, not the will (Lombard, 'Sent.,' III) ; since when a man refrains from some sins through fear of being punished, his will does not shrink simply from sin, as does the will of a man who refrains from sin through love of righteousness: and hence the New Law, which is the law of love, is said to restrain the will.

"Nevertheless there were some in the state of the Old Testament who, having charity and the grace of the Holy Ghost, looked chiefly to spiritual and eternal promises: and in this respect they belonged to the New Law. In like manner in the New Testament there are some carnal men who have not yet attained to the perfection of the New Law; and these it was necessary, even under the New Testament, to lead to virtuous action by the fear of punishment and by temporal promises.

"But although the Old Law contained precepts of charity, nevertheless it did not confer the Holy Ghost 'by Whom charity . . . is spread abroad in our hearts' (Romans 5:5)."

Ibid., Q. CVII, Art. I.

f. "The sermon which our Lord delivered on the mountain contains the whole process of forming the life of a Christian. Therein man's interior movements are ordered; because, after declaring that his end is Beatitude, and after commending the authority of the Apostles, through whom the teaching of the Gospel was to be promulgated, He orders man's interior movements, first in regard to man himself, secondly in regard to his neighbor.

"This He does in regard to man himself in two ways, corresponding to man's two interior movements in respect of any prospective action, viz., volition of what has to be done, and intention of the end. Wherefore, in the first place, He directs man's will in respect of the various precepts of the Law: by prescribing that man should refrain not merely from those external works that are evil in themselves, but also from [the corresponding] internal acts and from the occasions of evil deeds. In the second place He directs man's intention, by teaching that in our good works we should seek neither human praise nor worldly riches, which is to lay up treasures on earth.

"Afterward He directs man's interior movement in respect of his neighbor, by forbidding us, on the one hand, to judge him rashly, unjustly or presumptuously; and on the other, to entrust him too readily with sacred things if he be unworthy.

"Lastly, He teaches us how to fulfil the teaching of the Gospel; viz., by imploring the help of God; by striving to enter by the narrow door of perfect virtue; and by being wary lest we be led astray by evil influences. Moreover, He declares that we must observe His commandments, and that it is not enough to make profession of faith, or to work miracles, or merely to hear His words."

Ibid., Q. CVIII, Art. III.

g. "The difference between a counsel and a commandment is that a commandment implies obligation, whereas a counsel is left to the option of the one to whom it is given. Consequently in the New Law, which is the law of liberty, counsels are added to the commandments and are not in the Old Law, which is the law of bondage. We must therefore understand the commandments of the New Law to have been given about matters that are necessary to gain the end of eternal bliss, to which end the New Law brings us forthwith: but that the counsels are about matters that render the gaining of this end more assured and expeditious."

Ibid., Art. IV.

h. "The New Law fulfils the Old by justifying men through the power of Christ's Passion. This is what the Apostle says (Romans 8:3, 4). And in this respect, the New Law gives what the Old Law promised according to 2 Corinthians 1:20. Again, in this respect, it also fulfils what the Old Law foreshadowed. . . . Wherefore the New Law is called the law of reality; whereas the Old Law is called the law of shadow or of figure."

Ibid., Q. CVII, Art. II.

i. " 'Thou shalt love the Lord thy God with thy whole heart, and with thy whole soul, and with thy whole mind'; and 'thou shalt love thy neighbor as thyself' (Matt. 22:37-39). Natural philosophy is here, since all the causes of all natural things are in God the Creator. Ethics are here, since a good honest life is not formed otherwise than by loving as they should be loved those things which we ought to love, namely, God and our neighbor. Logic is here, since God alone is the truth and the light of the rational soul. Here too is laudable security for the commonwealth; for a state is neither founded nor preserved perfectly save in the foundation and by the bond of faith and of firm concord, when the highest common good is loved by all, and this highest and truest thing is God; when, too, men love one another in Him with absolute sincerity; since they love one another for His sake from whom they cannot hide the real character of their love."

St. Augustine, "Epist.," CXXXVII, v, 17.

F. BIBLICAL BACKGROUND

Holy Church, authorized by Jesus to be the Infallible Teacher of Doctrine, tells us that Christ's principles as unfolded in the Scriptures are inspired. In other words, Holy Church teaches us that the Bible, the Old and New Testaments, is the inspired word of God. This being true, we as Catholics should find special delight in studying the Life of Christ from this inspired Book.

And is it not regrettable that such large numbers of our older children have been trained to read the glorious facts of Jesus' Life only from cold, uninspired Bible Histories? The effect of this procedure has been that large numbers of our adults have never experienced the delight which reading the inspired Book gives.

In this section, selected Bible texts are presented which if assimilated by the teacher in some measure, will help to bring delight into his teaching of Book Three.

1.   The Mother of God's Own Son

a. Genesis 3:15

"I will put enmities between thee and the woman . . . and thou shalt lie in wait for her heel."

b. Canticles 4:7

"Thou art all fair, O my love, and there is not a spot in thee."

Canticles 6:8

"One is my dove, my perfect one. . . . "

c. Isaias 7:14

" . . . Behold a virgin shall conceive and bear a Son. . . . "

d. Luke 1:26-35

"And in the sixth month, the angel Gabriel was sent from God . . . to a virgin. . . . And the virgin's name was Mary. . . . And the angel said . . . : Fear not, Mary, for thou hast found grace with God. Behold thou shalt conceive in thy womb, and shalt bring forth a Son; and thou shalt call His name Jesus. . . . And therefore also the Holy which shall be born of thee shall be called the Son of God."

Luke 1:41-44

"... And she [Elizabeth] cried out with a loud voice, and said: Blessed art thou among women, and blessed is the fruit of thy womb. ... Behold as soon as the voice of thy salutation sounded in my ears, the infant in my womb leaped for joy."

Luke 1:45-55

"And Mary said: My soul doth magnify the Lord. ... Because He that is mighty hath done great things to me; ...."

Luke 11:27

"... Blessed is the womb that bore Thee, and the paps that gave Thee suck."

e. Galatians 4:4

"... God sent His Son, made of a woman."

f. Apocalypse 12:1

"And a great sign appeared in heaven: A woman clothed with the sun, and the moon under her feet, and on her head a crown of twelve stars."

2. St. Joseph

a. Matthew 1:18, 25

"... When as His [Christ's] Mother Mary was espoused to Joseph, ... she was found with child, of the Holy Ghost. Whereupon Joseph her husband, being a JUST MAN, ... he knew her not till she brought forth her first-born Son: and he called His name Jesus."

b. Luke 3:23

"And Jesus Himself was beginning about the age of thirty years; being (as it was supposed) the son of Joseph. ... "

c. John 6:41, 42

"The Jews therefore murmured ... and they said: Is not this Jesus, the son of Joseph, whose father and mother we know? How then saith he, I came down from heaven?"

3. The Baby Jesus

a. Luke 2:4-20

"And Joseph also went up from Galilee out of the city of Nazareth into Judea, to the city of David, which is called Bethlehem: because he was of the house and family of David, to be enrolled with
Mary, his espoused wife, who was with child. . . . And she brought
forth her first-born Son, and wrapped Him up in swaddling clothes,
and laid Him in a manger. . . . And there were in the same country shepherds watching . . . and behold an angel of the Lord stood by them.
. . . And the angel said to them: Fear not; for behold, I bring you good
tidings of great joy. . . . For this day is born to you a Saviour, Who
is Christ the Lord. . . . "

b. Matthew 2:1-11

"When Jesus therefore was born in Bethlehem of Juda, . . . there
came wise men from the east to Jerusalem, saying, Where is He that is
born King of the Jews? . . . In Bethlehem of Juda. For so it is written
by the prophet [Micheas 5:2]: 'And thou Bethlehem. . . . 'And entering
into the house, they found the Child with Mary His Mother, and falling down they adored Him; and opening their treasures they offered
Him gifts. . . . "

Matthew 2:13, 14

"And after they [the wise men] were departed, behold an angel
of the Lord appeared in sleep to Joseph, saying: Arise, and take the
Child and His Mother, and fly into Egypt: and be there until I shall
tell thee. . . . "

Matthew 2:16, 18

" . . . Herod perceiving that he was deluded by the wise men was
exceeding angry; and sending killed all the men children that were in
Bethlehem, and in all the borders thereof from two years old and
under. . . . "

*It would be necessary to possess some knowledge of the entire Bible
in order to have a complete background for teaching the Life of Christ.*

4. Jesus' Life and Cruel Death

a. Matthew 5, 6, 7

The Sermon on the Mount.

Matthew 7:28, 29

"And it came to pass when Jesus had fully ended these words, the people were in admiration at His doctrine. For He was teaching them as one having power...."

Matthew 8:1

"And when He was come down from the mountain great multitudes followed Him."

Matthew 8:2-34

Miracles.

Matthew 26:36-68

The Passion.

Matthew 27:1-66

The Passion, death and burial.

b. Mark 1:9-45

The baptism of Christ.
The Temptation in the desert.
The Calling of the Apostles.
Miracles.

Mark 6:1-13

"... And many hearing Him were in admiration at His doctrine, saying: How came this Man by all these things? And what wisdom is this that is given to Him, and such mighty works as are wrought by His hands?... He went through the villages round about teaching. And He called the Twelve...."

Mark 6:31-56

"... And Jesus going out saw a great multitude: and He had compassion on them, because they were as sheep not having a shepherd, And He began to teach them many things. And when the day was now far spent, His disciples came to Him saying: This is a desert place. ... And He answering said to them: Give you them to eat.... And they that did eat were five thousand men.... And whithersoever He entered, into towns or into villages or cities, they laid the sick in the streets ... and as many as touched Him were made whole."

Mark 14:26-72

The Passion.

Mark 15:1-47

The Passion, death and burial.

c. **Luke 2:51**

"And He went down with them, and came to Nazareth, and was subject to them."

Luke 10:1-20

"And after these things the Lord appointed also other seventy-two. ... And He said to them: ... Go: Behold I send you as lambs among wolves.... And the seventy-two returned with joy saying: Lord, the devils also are subject to us in Thy name...."

Luke 11:1-14

Teaching on prayer; the "Our Father."

Luke 18:15-17

"And they brought unto Him also infants.... Jesus ... said: ... Whosoever shall not receive the kingdom of God as a child, shall not enter into it."

Luke 21:37, 38

"And in the daytime He was teaching in the Temple; but at night, going out, He abode in the mount that is called Olivet, and all the people came early in the morning to Him in the temple to hear Him."

Luke 22:39-71

The Passion.

Luke 23:1-56

The Passion, death and burial.

d. **John 1:1-18**

"In the beginning was the Word.... No man hath seen God at any time: ... the only-begotten Son Who is in the bosom of the Father, He hath declared Him."

John 3:1-36

"... Rabbi, we know that Thou art come a teacher from God; for no man can do these signs which Thou dost, unless God be with him. Jesus answered, and said to him: ... He that believeth in the Son hath life everlasting; but he that believeth not the Son shall not see life; but the wrath of God abideth on him."

John 11:27

"She [Martha] saith to Him: Yea, Lord, I have believed that Thou art Christ the Son of the living God, Who art come into this world."

John 11:47-53

"The chief priests, therefore, and the Pharisees, gathered a council, and said: What do we, for this Man doth many miracles? If we let Him alone so, all will believe in Him; ... But one of them named Caiphas ... prophesied that Jesus should die for the nation. ... From that day therefore they devised to put Him to death."

John 18:1-40

The Passion.

John 19:1-42

The Passion, death and burial.

5. Jesus Is God

a. Matthew 16:21

"From that time Jesus began to show to His disciples that He must go to Jerusalem, and suffer many things from the ancients and scribes and chief priests, and be put to death, and the third day rise again."

Matthew 17:22

"... They shall kill Him and the third day He shall rise again. ..."

Matthew 20:18, 19

"Behold we go up to Jerusalem, and the Son of Man shall be betrayed ... and crucified, and the third day He shall rise again."

Matthew 26:31, 32

"Then Jesus saith to them: ... After I shall be risen again I will go before you into Galilee."

Matthew 27:64

"Command therefore the sepulchre to be guarded until the third day: lest perhaps His disciples come and steal Him away, and say to the people: He is risen from the dead; and the last error shall be worse than the first."

Matthew 28:1-15

The Resurrection.

b. Mark 9:8, 9

"... He charged them not to tell any man what things they had seen, till the Son of Man shall be risen again from the dead. ..."

Mark 16:1-16

The Resurrection.

c. Luke 24:1-49

The Resurrection.

d. John 2:18-22

"Jesus ... said. ... Destroy this temple, and in three days I will raise it up. ... When therefore He was risen again from the dead, His disciples remembered that He had said this, and they believed the Scripture, and the word that Jesus had said."

John 20:1-20

The Resurrection.

e. I Corinthians 15:3-8

"... Christ died for our sins. ... He was buried and ... He rose again the third day. ... He was seen by Cephas ... and last of all He was seen also by me. ..."

I Corinthians 15:20

"But now Christ is risen from the dead, the first fruits of them that sleep."

6. The Holy Ghost

The Holy Ghost is God

a. I Corinthians 2:10, 11

"... For the Spirit searcheth all things, yea, the deep things of God. ... So the things also that are of God no man knoweth but the Spirit of God."

I Corinthians 6:11

" . . . But you are sanctified, but you are justified in the name of our Lord Jesus Christ, and the Spirit of our God."

I Corinthians 6:20

"For you are bought with a great price. Glorify and bear God in your body."

The Holy Ghost Proceeds from the Father

a. Matthew 10:20

"For it is not you that speak, but THE SPIRIT OF YOUR FATHER that speaketh in you."

b. John 14:16

"And I will ask the Father and HE SHALL GIVE YOU AN-OTHER PARACLETE that He may abide with you forever."

John 14:26

"But the Paraclete, THE HOLY GHOST, WHOM THE FATHER WILL SEND in my name, He will teach you all things, and bring all things to your mind, whatsoever I shall have said to you."

John 15:26

"But when the Paraclete cometh, Whom I will send you from the Father, THE SPIRIT OF TRUTH, WHO PROCEEDETH FROM THE FATHER, He shall give testimony of Me."

The Holy Ghost Proceeds Also from the Son

a. Acts 16:7

"And when they were come into Mysia, they attempted to go into Bithynia and THE SPIRIT OF JESUS suffered them not."

b. Galatians 4:6

"And because you are sons, God hath sent THE SPIRIT OF HIS SON into your hearts, crying: Abba, Father."

c. Philippians 1:19

"For I know that this shall fall out to me unto salvation, through your prayer, and the supply of THE SPIRIT OF JESUS CHRIST."

d. I Peter 1:11

"Searching what or what manner of time THE SPIRIT OF CHRIST in them did signify."

The Holy Ghost is Sent by the Son

a. Luke 24:49

"And I SEND THE PROMISE OF MY FATHER UPON YOU: but stay you in the city, till you be endued with power from on high."

b. John 15:26

"But when the Paraclete cometh WHOM I WILL SEND YOU FROM THE FATHER, the Spirit of truth. . . . "

John 16:7

"But I tell you the truth: it is expedient to you that I go: for if I go not, the Paraclete will not come to you; but if I go, I WILL SEND HIM TO YOU."

c. John 20:22

"When He had said this, He breathed on them; and He said to them: RECEIVE YE THE HOLY GHOST."

When Any Soul Shares in God's Own Love and Truth, the Holy Ghost Dwells There

a. John 14:17

"THE SPIRIT OF TRUTH, Whom the world cannot receive, because it seeth Him not, nor knoweth Him: but you shall know Him: because HE SHALL ABIDE WITH YOU AND SHALL BE IN YOU."

John 14:26

"But the Paraclete, THE HOLY GHOST . . . WILL TEACH YOU ALL THINGS, AND BRING ALL THINGS TO YOUR MIND whatsoever I shall have said to you."

John 16:13

"But when He, THE SPIRIT OF TRUTH, is come, HE WILL TEACH YOU ALL TRUTH. For He shall not speak of Himself; but what things soever He shall hear, He shall speak; and the things that are to come, He shall show you."

b. Acts 1:5-8

"For John indeed baptized with water, but you shall be baptized with the Holy Ghost. . . . YOU SHALL RECEIVE THE POWER OF THE HOLY GHOST COMING UPON YOU, and you shall be witnesses unto Me in Jerusalem. . . . "

Acts 2:1-4

"And when the days of the Pentecost were accomplished, they were all together in one place: . . . And THEY WERE ALL FILLED WITH THE HOLY GHOST, and they began to speak with divers tongues according as the Holy Ghost gave them to speak."

c. Romans 5:5

"And hope confoundeth not: because THE CHARITY OF GOD IS POURED FORTH IN OUR HEARTS, BY THE HOLY GHOST, Who is given to us."

Romans 8:9, 11

"But you are not in the flesh, but in the spirit, if so be that the Spirit of God dwell in you. Now if any man have not the Spirit of Christ, he is none of His. . . . And if the Spirit of Him that raised up Jesus from the dead dwell in you; HE THAT RAISED UP JESUS CHRIST FROM THE DEAD, SHALL QUICKEN ALSO YOUR MORTAL BODIES, BECAUSE OF HIS SPIRIT THAT DWELLETH IN YOU."

d. I Corinthians 6:19

"Or know you not that YOUR MEMBERS ARE THE TEMPLE OF THE HOLY GHOST WHO IS IN YOU, Whom you have from God; and you are not your own?"

e. 2 Corinthians 1:21, 22

"Now He that confirmeth us with you in Christ, and that hath anointed us is God: WHO ALSO HATH SEALED US, AND GIVEN THE PLEDGE OF THE SPIRIT IN OUR HEARTS."

f. Galatians 4:6

"And because you are sons, GOD HATH SENT THE SPIRIT OF HIS SON INTO YOUR HEARTS crying: Abba, Father."

g. Thessalonians 4:8

"Therefore he that despiseth these things despiseth not man, but God, WHO ALSO HATH GIVEN HIS HOLY SPIRIT IN US."

h. 2 Timothy 1:14

"Keep the good things committed to thy trust by THE HOLY GHOST, WHO DWELLETH IN US."

i. Titus 3:5, 6

"... He saved us by the laver of regeneration, and renovation of THE HOLY GHOST, WHOM HE HATH POURED FORTH UPON US ... THROUGH JESUS CHRIST, OUR SAVIOUR."

7. The Holy Trinity

a. Matthew 3:16, 17

"And Jesus being baptized, ... the heavens were opened to Him: and He saw the Spirit of God descending as a dove and coming upon Him. And behold a voice from heaven saying: This is My beloved Son, in Whom I am well pleased."

Matthew 28:19

"Going therefore, teach ye all nations; baptizing them in the name of the Father, and of the Son, and of the Holy Ghost."

b. Luke 1:32-35

"He shall be great and shall be called the Son of the Most High. . . .

"And the angel answering, said to her [Mary]: The Holy Ghost shall come upon thee. . . . And therefore also the Holy which shall be born of thee shall be called the Son of God."

c. John 14:26

"But the Paraclete, the Holy Ghost, Whom the Father will send in My name, He will teach you all things."

d. 2 Corinthians 13:13

"The grace of our Lord Jesus Christ, and the charity of God, and the communication of Holy Ghost be with you all. Amen."

e. 1 Peter 1:2

"According to the foreknowledge of God the Father, unto the sanctification of the Spirit, unto obedience and sprinkling of the blood of Jesus Christ: Grace unto you and peace be multiplied."

f. 1 John 5:7

"And there are Three Who give testimony in heaven, the Father, the Word, and the Holy Ghost. And these Three are one."

8.   Stories Telling How to Be Like Jesus

Jesus Our Model: Prayer

a. Matthew 6:5, 6

"Amen, I say to you: When thou shalt pray, enter into thy chamber, and having shut the door, PRAY TO THY FATHER IN SECRET: and thy Father, Who seeth in secret, will repay thee."

b. Matthew 14:23

" . . . He went into a mountain alone to PRAY. . . . "

Matthew 21:21, 22

"Jesus . . . said to them: . . . And all things whatsoever you shall ask IN PRAYER, believing, you shall receive."

Matthew 26:36, 44

" . . . He said to His disciples: Sit you here, till I go yonder and PRAY. . . . And going a little further, He fell upon His face, PRAYING. . . . AGAIN THE SECOND TIME, HE WENT AND PRAYED. . . . And leaving them, He went again: and HE PRAYED THE THIRD TIME. . . . "

c. Mark 14:32-39

"And they came to a farm called Gethsemani. And He saith to His disciples: Sit you here, while I PRAY. . . . And He cometh, and findeth them sleeping. And He saith to Peter: . . . WATCH YE AND PRAY that you enter not into temptation."

d. Luke 5:16

"And He retired into the desert and PRAYED."

Luke 6:12, 13

"And it came to pass in those days, that HE WENT OUT INTO A MOUNTAIN TO PRAY, and He passed the whole night in the prayer of God. And when day was come He called unto Him His disciples; and He chose twelve of them (whom also He named Apostles)."

Luke 9:18

"And it came to pass, as HE WAS ALONE PRAYING, . . . "

Luke 11:2-14

"And He said to them: When YOU PRAY say: Father, hallowed be Thy name.... And I say to you, ask, and it shall be given you: seek, and you shall find: knock, and it shall be opened to you. FOR EVERYONE THAT ASKETH, RECEIVETH...."

Luke 22:43

"And there appeared to Him an angel from heaven, strengthening Him. And being in an agony HE PRAYED the longer."

e. John 17:9, 20

"... I PRAY not for the world, but for them whom Thou hast given Me: because they are Thine.... And not for them only do I PRAY, but for them also who through their word shall believe in Me...."

Jesus Our Model: All-Holy

a. Ecclesiasticus 30:15

"Health of the soul in HOLINESS of justice is better than all gold and silver...."

b. Luke 1:35

"... THE HOLY WHICH SHALL BE BORN OF THEE shall be called the Son of God."

Luke 6:19

"And all the multitude sought to touch Him, for VIRTUE WENT OUT FROM HIM and healed all."

c. John 1:14

"And the Word was made flesh and dwelt among us, ... FULL OF GRACE AND TRUTH."

John 8:29

"... I do always the things that please Him."

d. Acts 3:14

"But you denied the HOLY ONE and the Just...."

Acts 4:29, 30

"And now, Lord, ... grant unto Thy servants that with all confidence they may speak Thy word. By stretching forth Thy hand to cures, and signs, and wonders to be done by the name of THY HOLY SON Jesus."

Acts 10:38

" ... Jesus of Nazareth: how GOD ANOINTED HIM WITH THE HOLY GHOST, and with power, Who went about doing good, and healing all that were oppressed by the devil, for God was with Him."

e. Ephesians 1:4

"As He chose us in Him before the foundation of the world, that we should be HOLY and unspotted in His sight in charity."

f. Colossians 1:19, 21, 22

"Because in Him it hath well pleased the Father that ALL FULNESS SHOULD DWELL. And ... through death to present you HOLY ... before Him."

Colossians 2:3, 9, 10

"In Whom [Christ Jesus] are hid all the treasures of wisdom and knowledge. For in Him dwelleth ALL THE FULNESS OF THE GODHEAD, corporeally; and you are filled in Him, Who is the head of all principality and power."

g. Hebrews 7:26

"For it was fitting that we should have such a High Priest, HOLY, innocent, undefiled, separated from sinners, and made higher than the heavens."

Hebrews 12:14

"Follow peace with all men, AND HOLINESS: without which no man shall see God."

h. I Peter 1:15, 16

"But according to Him that hath called you, WHO IS HOLY, be you also in all manner of conversation holy. Because it is written: You shall be holy, for I am holy."

i. I John 3:2, 3

" ... We shall be like to Him because we shall see Him as He is. And everyone that hath this hope in Him sanctifieth himself, as He also is HOLY."

Jesus Our Model: Shows Love to Everyone; Teaches
the Doctrine of Showing Love to Others

a. Matthew 5:43-48

"You have heard that it hath been said, Thou shalt love thy neighbor and hate thy enemy. But I say to you, LOVE YOUR ENEMIES; do good to them that hate you. . . . For if you love them that love you, what reward shall you have? . . . Be you therefore perfect, as also your heavenly Father is perfect."

Matthew 7:16, 17

"By their fruits you shall know them. Do men gather grapes of thorns or figs of thistles? Even so, every good tree bringeth forth good fruit, and the evil tree bringeth forth evil fruit."

Matthew 10:42

"And whosoever shall give to drink to one of these little ones a cup of cold water only in the name of a disciple, amen I say to you, he shall not lose his reward."

Matthew 11:4, 5

"Jesus making answer said to them: Go and relate to John what you have heard and seen. The blind see, the lame walk, the lepers are cleansed, the deaf hear, the dead rise again, the poor have the Gospel preached to them."

The greater number of Jesus' miracles were performed to show love, and could be used as illustrations here.

b. Luke 7:47, 48

"Many sins are forgiven her [Mary Magdalen] BECAUSE SHE HATH LOVED MUCH. . . . And He said to her: Thy sins are forgiven thee."

Luke 23:33-43

"And when they were come to the place which is called Calvary, they crucified Him there; and the robbers, one on the right hand, and the other on the left. . . . And one of those robbers . . . blasphemed Him. . . . But the other . . . rebuked him saying: . . . We indeed [suffer] justly, for we receive the due reward of our deeds. . . . And he said to Jesus: Lord, remember me when Thou shalt come into Thy kingdom. And Jesus said to him: Amen I say to thee, this day thou shalt be with Me in paradise."

c. **John 10:15**

"I lay down My life for My sheep."

John 11:3, 35, 36

"His [Lazarus'] sisters therefore sent to Him saying: Lord, behold, he whom Thou lovest is sick.... And Jesus wept. The Jews therefore said: BEHOLD HOW HE LOVED HIM."

John 13:1

"... Having loved His own who were in the world, HE LOVED THEM UNTO THE END."

John 15:9

"As the Father hath loved Me, I also have loved you. ABIDE IN MY LOVE."

John 15:13

"GREATER LOVE THAN THIS NO MAN HATH, that a man lay down his life for his friends."

d. **Galatians 2:20**

"I live in the faith of the Son of God, WHO LOVED ME, and delivered Himself for me."

e. **Ephesians 3:19**

"To know also THE CHARITY OF CHRIST which surpasseth all knowledge...."

Ephesians 5:1, 2

"Be ye therefore followers of God, as most dear children; and WALK IN LOVE as Christ also hath loved us and hath delivered Himself for us...."

f. **I John 3:16**

"In this we have known the CHARITY OF GOD, because He hath laid down His life for us and we ought to lay down our lives for the brethren."

Jesus Our Model: Truth

a. Psalm 24:4, 5

"Show, O Lord, Thy ways to me, . . . Direct me in Thy TRUTH and teach me."

Psalm 84:12

"TRUTH IS SPRUNG OUT OF THE EARTH: and justice hath looked down from heaven."

Psalm 118:30

"I have chosen the WAY OF TRUTH. . . . "

Psalm 145:5, 7

"Blessed is he WHO KEEPETH TRUTH forever. . . . "

b. Ecclesiasticus 15:8

". . . MEN THAT SPEAK TRUTH shall be found with her [Wisdom] and shall advance, even till they come to the sight of God."

c. John 1:17

" . . . Grace and TRUTH came by Jesus Christ."

John 14:6

"Jesus saith: I am the Way and the TRUTH and the Life."

John 17:19

"For them do I sanctify Myself, that they also may be sanctified in TRUTH."

d. Ephesians 4:15

"But DOING THE TRUTH IN CHARITY, we may in all things grow up in Him Who is the head, even Christ."

Ephesians 4:25

"Wherefore putting away lying, SPEAK YE THE TRUTH every man with his neighbor, for we are members one of another."

e. 1 John 5:6

" . . . It is the spirit which testifieth that CHRIST IS THE TRUTH."

Jesus Our Model: Obedience

a. Matthew 26:39

" ... Nevertheless not as I will but as Thou wilt."

b. Luke 2:51

" ... He ... was subject to them."

Luke 6:46, 47

"And why call you Me, Lord, Lord; and do not the things which I say? Everyone that cometh to Me, and heareth My words, and doth them, I will show you to whom he is like."

Luke 20:25

"And He said to them: Render therefore to Caesar the things that are Caesar's: and to God the things that are God's."

c. John 4:34

" ... My meat is to do the will of Him that sent Me, that I may perfect His work."

John 6:38

"Because I came down from heaven, not to do My own will, but the will of Him that sent Me."

John 14:31

"But that the world may know that I love the Father: and as the Father hath given Me commandment, SO DO I. ... "

John 15:10

"If you keep My commandments, you shall abide in My love; as I also have kept My Father's commandments and do abide in His love."

d. Romans 5:19

"For as by the disobedience of one man many were made sinners; so also by the obedience of one, many shall be made just."

e. Philippians 2:8

"He humbled Himself, becoming obedient unto death, even to the death of the cross."

f. Colossians 3:17-23

"All whatsoever you do in word or in work, do all in the name of the Lord Jesus Christ.... Wives be subject to your husbands.... Husbands, love your wives.... Children, obey your parents in all things. ... Servants, obey in all things your masters.... Whatsoever you do, do it from the heart, as to the Lord, and not to men."

g. Hebrews 5:8, 9

"And whereas indeed He was the Son of God, He learned obedience by the things which He suffered: and being consummated, He became, to all that obey Him, the cause of eternal salvation."

Hebrews 10:7

"Then said I: Behold I come: in the head of the book it is written of Me that I should do Thy will, O God."

Jesus Our Model: Kind and Gentle

a. Matthew 4:23, 24

Jesus heals the sick.

Matthew 8:2-4

A miracle: the healing of the leper.

Matthew 8:5-13

A miracle: the healing of the centurion's servant.

Matthew 8:14, 15

A miracle: the healing of Peter's wife's mother.

Matthew 8:16, 17

Jesus casts out devils.

Matthew 14:14

Jesus heals the sick.

Matthew 15:32

Jesus' compassion on the multitude.

Matthew 20:30-34

A miracle: the healing of the blind men.

Matthew 26:48-50

"And he that betrayed Him gave them a sign saying: Whomsoever I shall kiss, that is He, hold Him fast. . . . And Jesus said to him: Friend, whereto art thou come? . . . "

b. Luke 7:11-16

A miracle: Jesus raises the widow's son to life.

Luke 7:37-50

The story of Mary Magdalen.

Luke 13:11-13

A miracle — the healing of an infirm woman.

Luke 22:54-62

St. Peter's denial of Jesus.

c. John 11:32-44

A miracle — the raising of Lazarus from the dead.

Jesus Our Model: Poverty of Spirit

a. Zacharias 9:9

" . . . Behold thy King will come to thee, the Just and Saviour: He is POOR. . . . "

b. Matthew 5:3

"BLESSED ARE THE POOR IN SPIRIT. . . . "

Matthew 6:25-34

From the Sermon on the Mount.

c. Luke 2:7

The Baby Jesus was laid in a manger.

Luke 6:20

"BLESSED ARE YE POOR. . . . "

Luke 9:58

" . . . The foxes have holes, and the birds of the air nests; but the Son of Man hath not where to lay His head."

d. 2 Corinthians 8:9

" . . . Our Lord Jesus Christ . . . being rich . . . became poor. . . . "

9. The Commandments of the Old and the New Law

a. Exodus 20

The Ten Commandments.

b. Leviticus 19:18

"Thou shalt love thy friend as thyself. I am the Lord."

c. Deuteronomy 5:1-22

The Ten Commandments.

Deuteronomy 6:4-7

"Hear, O Israel, the Lord our God is one Lord. THOU SHALT LOVE THE LORD THY GOD WITH THY WHOLE HEART, AND WITH THY WHOLE SOUL, AND WITH THY WHOLE STRENGTH. And these words which I command thee this day, shall be in thy heart: and thou shalt tell them to thy children, and thou shalt meditate upon them sitting in thy house, and walking on thy journey, sleeping and rising."

Deuteronomy 11:13-16

"If then you obey My commandments which I command you this day, that you love the Lord your God, and serve Him with all your heart, and with all your soul: He will give to your land the early rain. ... Beware lest perhaps your heart be deceived, and you depart from the Lord. ... "

d. Matthew 5:43, 44

"You have heard that it hath been said, Thou shalt love thy neighbor and hate thy enemy. But I say to you, Love your enemies: do good to them that hate you: and pray for them that persecute and calumniate you."

Matthew 22:37-40

"Jesus said to him: Thou shalt love the Lord thy God with thy whole heart, and with thy whole soul, and with thy whole mind. This is the greatest and the first commandment. And the second is like to this: Thou shalt love thy neighbor as thyself. ON THESE TWO COMMANDMENTS DEPEND THE WHOLE LAW AND THE PROPHETS."

e. Mark 12:29-31

" . . . The first commandment of all is, Hear O Israel: the Lord thy God is one God. And thou shalt love the Lord thy God, with thy whole heart, and with thy whole soul, and with thy whole mind, and with thy whole strength. This is the first commandment. And the second is like to it: Thou shalt love thy neighbor as thyself. THERE IS NO OTHER COMMANDMENT GREATER THAN THESE."

f. Luke 6:27, 28

"But I say to you that hear: Love your enemies, do good to them that hate you. Bless them that curse you, and pray for them that calumniate you."

Luke 10:27, 28

"He [Jesus] answering said: Thou shalt love the Lord thy God with thy whole heart, and with thy whole soul, and with all thy strength and with all thy mind: and thy neighbor as thyself. . . . This do and thou shalt live."

g. Romans 13:8-10

"Owe no man anything but to love one another. For he that loveth his neighbor hath fulfilled the law. For Thou shalt not commit adultery: Thou shalt not kill: Thou shalt not steal: Thou shalt not bear false witness: Thou shalt not covet: and if there be any other commandment, it is comprised in this word, Thou shalt love thy neighbor as thyself. The love of our neighbor worketh no evil: LOVE THERE-FORE IS THE FULFILLING OF THE LAW."

h. Galatians 5:14

"For all the law is fulfilled in one word: Thou shalt love thy neighbor as thyself."

i. James 2:8

"If then you fulfil the royal law, according to the Scriptures, Thou shalt love thy neighbor as thyself, you do well."

10.   The Mystical Body of Christ

a. Romans 12:3-17

"... So we, being many, are one body in Christ, and every one members one of another...."

b. I Corinthians 12:4-31

" ... Now you are — the body of Christ, and members of members...."

Other texts will be included in the Biblical background of Jesus' Church — Book Four, page 167.

BOOK FOUR
"The Holy Way, the Straight Way"

BASAL MATERIAL

FOR

DISCUSSING OR TEACHING

BOOK FOUR: "THE HOLY WAY, THE STRAIGHT WAY"

F. BIBLICAL BACKGROUND

Jesus' Church

The Holy Sacrifice of the Mass

Book Four:

"The Holy Way, the Straight Way"

A. INTRODUCTORY

Jesus' Church

The title of Book Four, "The Holy Way, the Straight Way," is taken from a prophecy of Isaias, chapter 35, verse 8. And since the prophecy refers to Jesus' Church, these words give to the child, from the very beginning of our teaching concerning Holy Church, THE RIGHT KEYNOTE.

In these troubled days it is very necessary to the child, in his path toward truth and holiness, that he know clearly why the Holy Catholic Church is the only sure guide — and why every man, woman and child should love this Church.

So, in our teaching, the first points that we must make sure are solidly established in the child's mind are, that

JESUS IS GOD'S OWN SON

and that

THE HOLY CATHOLIC CHURCH IS JESUS' CHURCH.

After that, the child must understand clearly the following two purposes for which God's Own Son established His Church:

1. That after He went back to His Father in heaven, the people, for love of whom He had given His Life, would still have a

TRUE GUIDE AND TEACHER;

2. That they would also have

A SURE WAY TO HAVE GOD'S LOVE AND TRUTH IN THEM.

And even a little child must be taught that IT IS THE POWER OF THE HOLY GHOST WHICH GUARDS JESUS' CHURCH, and that the power of the Holy Ghost is the greatest and most lasting power in the world.

The word "Infallibility" will be taught to the child in other lessons after the First Communion series, and at that time a more advanced development, based upon the promises of Jesus, will be presented to him.

The whole teaching concerning Jesus' Church should be STRONGLY MOTIVATED through an understanding of the great need which we have for Jesus' Church, and the entire lesson should be permeated with a background of HUMILITY and FAITH.

Above all, this important unit should end with such an abiding love for Jesus' Church as will lead to courage and sacrifice when there is need.

The Holy Sacrifice of the Mass

Too many Catholics perform the obligation of assisting at Holy Mass in a perfunctory way, and too many Catholics think only of the obligation angle of this pivotal point of all Catholic worship. They never grasp the rich idea that through the Holy Sacrifice of the Mass is offered the very greatest privilege, in the way of rendering to God adequate praise, thanksgiving and reparation, and the surest way of drawing down our Father's blessing and causing Him to look lovingly upon all that we do.

In presenting to the child, for the first time, teaching concerning Holy Mass, it would be well, it seems to me, to remember a psychological principle which I am sure comes within the realm of nearly everyone's experience. This is the principle which I have in mind:

If in one's younger days a happy emotional experience is closely associated with any event or teaching, years afterward, when perhaps the event is of little interest, and the teaching outgrown, THE PLEASING EMOTIONAL EXPERIENCE WILL ALWAYS COLOR THE MEMORY OF THIS EVENT OR TEACHING.

Following this psychological principle, the teaching concerning Holy Mass in Book Four is introduced through a story ending with a sacred charge which David's father, on his deathbed, gave to David. And this sacred charge bade David have a faithful love for Holy Mass all the days of his life.

It is very important that, at the first presentation of this unit, so vital in the child's life, Holy Mass should not seem complicated to him.

To lessen this difficulty, it seems both wise and practical to BEGIN the presentation with the solemn part of Holy Mass. In Book Four the words of the Consecration are taken from the Westminster version of the Bible, which are in the present tense. After the teaching concerning the solemn part of Holy Mass has been carefully given, the child can then be taught that Holy Church gives us the prayers before the Consecration JUST TO PREPARE OUR MINDS for the Great Sacrifice which is about to take place, and that in the prayers after Holy Communion WE OFFER THANKS to God for the great blessings which have been poured upon us during the time of the Eucharistic Sacrifice.

In order that the child may have a more intelligent understanding of the Holy Mass, teaching concerning THE DOCTRINE OF THE MYSTICAL BODY OF CHRIST should be given. But in these beginning lessons it is not necessary that the term, "Mystical Body of Christ," be used. In Book Four, this teaching is given on pages 35 and 36.

The Liturgy, which means so much in the lives of our Catholic people, proceeds from and is based upon an understanding of doctrine. And a foundation for living in accordance with the Liturgy of the Church should be laid in these very beginning lessons.

In connection with the teaching concerning Holy Mass in Book Four, pages 32-35, seeds of the Liturgy are sown, and appropriate Psalm verses are taught as prayers on page 17 of Book Six.

The important and fundamental idea of Official Sacrifice is not taught in these beginning lessons, but later in Book Three of "The Spiritual Way," the Holy Sacrifice of the Mass is studied from an older point of view, and a complete topic on "The Sacrifices of the Old Law" is then carefully presented.

B. DOCTRINAL TRUTHS PRESENTED TO THE CHILD IN BOOK FOUR WITH THE EXPECTATION THAT HE WILL UNDERSTAND AND APPRECIATE THEM IN ACCORDANCE WITH HIS MENTAL AGE:

That:

1. "The Holy Way, the Straight Way," is Jesus' Church;

2. Stability and Truth are in Jesus' Church;

3. Jesus' Church is not only the True Teacher, but also the Sure Way through which God's Grace may be received;

4. it is the Power of the Holy Ghost which guards Jesus' Church and will remain with it until the end of the world;

5. the Holy Catholic Church is Jesus' Church;

6. if we love Jesus, we will love the Church He left us;

7. the priestly dignity and power are very great;

8. in Holy Mass, at the Consecration, Jesus is present, offering His Life for us just as He did when He was dying on the Cross;

9. on the Cross Jesus was our great Highpriest, and at the Consecration in Holy Mass Jesus is also our great Highpriest;

10. we may bring greater blessings upon ourselves and others if, at the Consecration in Holy Mass when Jesus offers Himself to His Father for us, we also offer Jesus to His Father;

11. we show we love God ABOVE ALL if, at the Consecration, we ask Jesus to offer with His Life our lives and with His Love and Obedience our love and obedience.

12. our Heavenly Father turns toward us with special love when Jesus, the Great and Holy Head of Us All, is present during Holy Mass offering Himself for us;

13. when we receive Holy Communion we receive Jesus in the Holy Host.

C. GROWTH IN POWER TO BE EXPECTED IN THE CHILD AS A RESULT OF STUDYING BOOK FOUR:

Greater facility:

1. in loving Holy Church and in obeying the Commandments of Holy Church;

2. in serving Holy Church;

3. in sacrificing for Holy Church;

4. in understanding why we offer our prayers through Jesus;

5. in understanding the reason for obedience to the Church in all that pertains to Faith and Morals;

6. in understanding what takes place at the Consecration in Holy Mass, and the type of prayers to be said at that time;

7. in understanding what to do during the first and last parts of Holy Mass;

8. in making sacrifices in order to be present at Holy Mass.

D. PEDAGOGICAL STRUCTURE

The application of psychological principles to the teaching of Holy Church and Holy Mass is of paramount importance if we want our teaching to result in an understanding and love of Holy Church and Holy Mass.

The pedagogical principle of motivation should receive special attention in presenting these two important subjects, and this principle does vitalize the lessons concerning Holy Church and Holy Mass in Book Four of "A Little Child's First Communion."

But before considering the presentation of these units, the teacher himself must have a clear understanding concerning the meaning and value of official sacrifice in both the Old and the New Law, and the meaning of the Supernatural Headship of Jesus. For the understanding of these two vital points of doctrine, Holy Church and Holy Mass, is so important in the child's life that the teacher should be teaching from a very complete and rich background.

Superficiality in this teaching and the ignoring of psychological principles will deprive the child of the spiritual advantages resulting from a deep faith in the Church and a deep participation in the Mass.

The following outline will help the teacher to apply psychological principles to the teaching of these two units.

Teacher's Major Objective

To instil in the child-mind such clear teaching concerning the Holy Catholic Church and the Holy Mass as to create in his mind a deep love for these two most vital truths of our faith.

The introductory page presents to the child the theme of Book Four.

Exploration and Establishment of an Apperceptive Background for the New Knowledge

This part of the lesson is an exploration into the child's mind to discover what he already knows which would dovetail into the new subject-matter about to be presented and establish an appropriate apperceptive background for it.

Motivation

The motivation begins with the sentence, "Jesus knew that after He went back to His Father in heaven, the people would no longer be able to see or hear Him."

Presentation of New Knowledge

Generalizations

a. The Holy Catholic Church is the Church that Jesus left to keep on teaching God's Truth and bringing God's Grace to the people.

b. Jesus gave power to His Priests to offer the Holy Sacrifice of the Mass.

c. In Holy Mass at the Consecation Jesus is present offering to His Father FOR US His Life, His Sufferings and His cruel death with all of His great love and obedience as He did when He was dying upon the Cross.

Applications and Related Activities

E. THEOLOGICAL BACKGROUND

Probably no other two units of doctrine to be presented by the teacher will require such a comprehensive theological background on his part as the two units presented in Book Four — Holy Church and Holy Mass.

The teacher should study the following theological excerpts, for they will do much to give him the comprehensive reserve knowledge which is necessary in teaching these two units in such a way as to make them become forceful factors in the child's life.

1. Sacrifice the Most Excellent Act of Religion

a. "Among the means of bringing man into supernatural communication with God and the expected Redeemer, sacrifice already before the coming of Christ held a prominent place, yea, the very first place. As Abel even at the threshold of Paradise, so during the patriarchal age, Noe, Melchisedech, Abraham, Jacob, offered sacrifices to God and God graciously accepted them. Then God Himself through Moses most precisely and minutely regulated and prescribed the entire sacrificial rite of the Old Law."

Gihr, "The Holy Sacrifice of the Mass," p. 36.

b. "Sacrifice is the most exalted and perfect manner of honoring God, and therefore excels all other acts of worship. It also constitutes the principal act, and is the central point of the whole divine service. In this all agree, that man by the offering of sacrifice renders to God the highest possible honor and homage."

Ibid., p. 31.

c. "Sacrifice, that is, the transformation of the gift offered, is intended to represent symbolically that God possesses absolute authority and dominion over all things, and consequently, that man is essentially dependent upon God, belongs and is subject to Him, and therefore that he is bound and is ready to give and dedicate his life entirely to God. God is the Supreme Ruler, infinitely holy, the primal source of all being, and the last end to which all being should return, "that God may be all in all' (1 Cor. 15:28)."

Ibid., p. 28.

d. "Hence the offering up of sacrifice essentially aims to glorify God as the absolute Lord and supreme Legislator of all creatures, and this is to adore God."

Ibid., p. 29.

e. "Sacrifice is an act of worship which cannot be performed by anybody but a priest. He alone has been especially chosen, called and empowered; that is, only the priest can and may perform the office of sacrificer. Sacrifice and priesthood are inseparably connected: no sacrifice can exist without a priesthood, and no priesthood without a sacrifice."

Ibid., p. 30.

f. "The Old Law contained 'only the shadow of the good things to come,' that is, the heavenly gifts of grace which Christ acquired for us and which He entrusted to the Church; for this reason the ancient sacrifices were but shadows of the great atoning sacrifice of Redemption on Golgotha."

Ibid., p. 38.

2. The Fountain-Head of the Entire Priesthood

a. "God conferred upon him [Melchisedech] the honor of prefiguring the priesthood and the sacrifice of Jesus Christ, inasmuch as both are perpetuated in the New Covenant. Christ is called 'a Priest forever according to the order of Melchisedech' (Psalm 109)."

Ibid., p. 84.

b. "Christ is not said to be according to the order of Melchisedech as though the latter were a more excellent priest: but because he foreshadowed the excellence of Christ's over the Levitical priesthood."

St. Thomas Aquinas, "Summa Theologica,"
Part Three, First Number, Q. XXII, Art. VI.

c. "This consummation of Christ's sacrifice was foreshadowed in this, that the highpriest of the Old Law once a year entered into the Holy of Holies with the blood of a he-goat and a calf, as laid down (Leviticus 16:11), and yet he offered up the he-goat and calf not within the Holy of Holies, but without. In like manner Christ entered into the Holy of Holies — that is, into heaven — and prepared the way for us, that we might enter by the virtue of His blood, which He shed for us *on earth*."

Ibid., Art. V.

d. "A priest is set beween God and man. . . . Now Christ is the Fountainhead of the entire priesthood: for the priest of the Old Law was a figure of Him; while the priest of the New Law works in His person, according to 2 Cor. 2:10."

Ibid., Art. IV.

3. Jesus, the Supernatural and Spiritual Head of Mankind

a. "For as Adam was the father of the mortal life of all men, so was Christ the Father of the immortal life of the faithful. . . . As, therefore, Adam was the beginning or origin of the old world, so is Christ of the new and better world."

Cornelius à Lapide (St. Matthew 1:1).

b. "Jesus is the spiritual, supernatural Head of mankind; this constitutes the mystical body, for which Christ, the Head, offered satisfaction and gained merit. Christ is the second Adam; as such He superabundantly repaired what the first Adam had destroyed and corrupted."

Gihr, op. cit., p. 40.

c. "All who from the beginning of the world have been righteous have Christ for their Head. For they believed that He was to come, Whom we believe to have now come; and it was in faith of Him in Whose faith we have been made whole, that they were made whole also; so that He should be in His own person the head of the whole of the City of Jerusalem. And all the faithful from the beginning unto the end were included in the number, to whom the legions and the armies of the Angels were also joined, so that it might become one City under one King. . . ."

St. Augustine, "In Ps. XXXVI," Serm. iii, 4.

d. ". . . If we take the whole time of the world in general, Christ is the Head of all men. For, first and principally, He is the Head of such as are united to Him by glory; secondly, of those who are actually united to Him by charity; thirdly, of those who are actually united to Him by faith; fourthly, of those who are united to Him merely in potentiality, which is not yet reduced to act yet will be reduced to act according to Divine predestination; fifthly, of those who are united to Him in potentiality, which will never be reduced to act; such as those men existing in the world, who are not predestined, who, yet, on their departure from this world, wholly cease to be members of Christ, as being no longer in potentiality to be united to Christ."

St. Thomas Aquinas, loc. cit., Q. VIII, Art. III.

e. "This vicarious sacrifice the God-Man, Jesus Christ, offered, inasmuch as He, the Head of the human race, gave His life by a bloody death to present to God not merely a strictly equivalent or fully sufficient, but even a superabundant and overflowing, satisfaction for the sins of all mankind."

Gihr, op. cit., p. 39.

f. "Origen says ('Sup. Joan.,' 1:29) though various animals were offered up under the Law, yet the daily sacrifice, which was offered up
morning and evening, was a lamb, as appears from Numbers 38:3, 4.
By which it was signified that the offering up of the Lamb, i. e., Christ,
was the culminating sacrifice of all. Hence (John 1:29) it is said:
'Behold the Lamb of God,' etc."
                                    St. Thomas Aquinas, loc. cit., Q. XXII, Art. 3.

g. "As a lamb Christ was promised in the Old Law through figures and
prophets; as a lamb He was pointed out in the New Law by John
the Baptist and extolled by the Apostles. With marked preference
St. John in his mystical Revelations calls (about twenty-seven times) the
Son of God a Lamb."
                                    Gihr, op. cit., p. 717.

4. Jesus' Church

a. "To be a glorious Church not having spot nor wrinkle is the ultimate
end to which we are brought by the Passion of Christ."
                                    St. Thomas Aquinas, loc. cit., Q. VIII, Art. III.

b. "Our Lord Jesus Christ is as one whole, perfect man, both head and
body. We acknowledge the Head in that Man who was born of the
Virgin Mary, suffered under Pontius Pilate, was buried, rose from the
dead, ascended into heaven, sitteth at the right hand of the Father,
from thence we look for Him to come to judge the living and the
dead. This is the Head of the Church (Eph. 5:23). The Body of
this Head is the Church, not the Church of this country only, but of
the whole world; not that of this age only, but from Abel himself
down to those who shall to the end be born and shall believe in Christ,
the whole assembly of saints belonging to one City, which City is
Christ's Body, of which Christ is the Head."
                                    St. Augustine, "In Ps. XC," Serm. ii, 1.

c. "As the whole Church is termed one mystic Body from its likeness to
the natural body of a man, which in divers members has divers acts,
as the Apostle teaches (Rom. 12 and 1 Cor. 12), so likewise Christ
is called the Head of the Church from a likeness with the human
head, in which we may consider three things — viz., order, perfection and power. . . .
    "Now these three things belong spiritually to Christ. First, on
account of His nearness to God His grace is the highest and first,
though not in time, according to Romans 8:29. . . . Secondly, He had
perfection as regards the fulness of all graces, according to John 1:14.

... Thirdly, He has the power of bestowing grace on all the members of the Church, according to John 1:16. Of His fulness we have all received. And thus it is plain that Christ is fittingly called the Head of the Church."

St. Thomas Aquinas, loc. cit., Q. VIII, Art. I.

d. "The head has a manifest preëminence over the other exterior members; but the heart has a certain hidden influence. And hence the Holy Ghost is likened to the heart, since He invisibly quickens and unifies the Church, but Christ is likened to the Head in His invisible nature, in which man is set over man."

Ibid.

e. "A multitude ordained to one end, with distinct acts and duties may be metaphorically called one body. But it is manifest that both men and angels are ordained to one end, which is the glory of the Divine fruition. Hence the mystical body of the Church consists not only of men but angels. Now of all this multitude Christ is the Head, since He is nearer God, and shares His gifts more fully, not only than man, but even than angels; and of His influence not only men but even angels partake, since it is written [Ephesians 1:20].... Therefore Christ is not only the Head of men but of angels. Hence we read (Matthew 4:11) that 'angels came and ministered to Him.' "

Ibid., Art. IV.

f. "Grace was received by the soul of Christ in the highest way; and therefore from this preëminence of grace which He received, it is from Him that this grace is bestowed on others; and this belongs to the nature of head. Hence the personal grace whereby the soul of Christ is justified, is essentially the same as His grace, as He is the Head of the Church, and justifies others; but there is a distinction of reason between them."

Ibid., Art. V.

g. "I say therefore that the efficacy of the Sacrament is one thing, the efficacy of prayer is another. For a sacrament derives its efficacy 'ex opere operato,' but prayer 'ex opere operantis,' from the sanctity and character of him who prays. And therefore if a sinner (a heretic, e. g.) baptizes, this sacrament is valid, and derives its efficacy from the institution of Christ, Who confers grace by the Sacrament. For Christ is the original author of Baptism, Who baptizes by His ministers as by instruments. Besides, though God hears not the prayers of a sinner as a private person, yet He hears the prayers of the same person in his public capacity, because he is a minister of the Church. For the Church is holy, as having Christ as its holy Head, and as having many faithful and holy members, to whose prayers God hearkens."

Cornelius à Lapide (St. John 9:31).

h. "The head not only influences the members interiorly, but also governs them exteriorly, directing their actions to an end. Hence it may be said that anyone is the head of a multitude either as regards both — i. e., by interior influence and exterior governance — and thus Christ is the Head of the Church, as was stated; or as regards exterior governance, and thus every prince or prelate is head of the multitide subject to him."

St. Thomas Aquinas, loc. cit., Q. VIII, Art. VII.

i. "The Church is spread throughout the whole world: all nations have the Church. Let no one deceive you; it is the true, it is the Catholic Church. Christ we have not seen, but we have her; let us believe as regards Him. The Apostles on the contrary saw Him, they believed as regards her. . . . They saw Christ, they believed in the Church which they did not see; and we who see the Church, let us believe in Christ, Whom we do not yet see."

St. Augustine, "Serm.," CCXXXVIII, 3.

j. "Hold this fast and keep it entirely fixed in your memory, as children of the Church's training and of the Catholic faith, that you may perceive Christ to be the Head and the Body, and the same Christ to be also the Word of God, the Only-Begotten, equal to the Father, and so may see how great is the grace whereby you pertain to God, that He, Who is one with the Father, has willed to be one with us. . . . Christ and the Church are two in one flesh. The 'two' you must refer to the distance of His Majesty from us. Clearly there are two. For we are not also the Word; we are not also God in the beginning with God: we are not also He by Whom all things were made (John 1:1-3)."

St. Augustine, "In Ps. CXLII," 3.

k. "THE CATHOLIC CHURCH IS THE GREAT INSTITUTE OF SALVATION, FOUNDED BY CHRIST FOR THE ENTIRE WORLD AND FOR ALL TIME; as such she has the sublime mission and task to continue and accomplish throughout all ages the work of Christ's redemption by the conversion and salvation of all nations. God wills that all men by means of the Church and in the Church should receive heavenly light and life and come to the knowledge of the truth and be saved (1 Timothy 2:4). For this purpose the Lord is and remains with His Church; in her He lives and acts all days until the end of the world. In sacramental truth and reality the God-Man continues always His mediatorship on earth by the ministry of His Church. AS HE REDEEMED MANKIND ESPECIALLY BY THE BLOODY SACRIFICE OF THE CROSS, SO HE CARRIES OUT THE WORK OF REDEMPTION IN HIS CHURCH CHIEFLY BY THE UNBLOODY SACRIFICE OF THE ALTAR. . . ."

Gihr, op. cit., p. 192.

5. The New Law: from the Synagogue to the Church

a. "The offering of the bloody Sacrifice of the Cross constitutes the conclusion and crowning of the earthly, as well as the foundation of the heavenly, activity and efficacy of Christ for the salvation of mankind. In the Sacrifice of the Cross all sacrifices prior to the coming of Christ have their fulfilment and by means of it have attained their end.

"On the Cross there was but one sacrifice (*hostia singularis*) offered to God for the redemption of the world, and the death of Christ, the true sacrificial Lamb, announced so many centuries in advance, placed the children of promise in the liberty of faith. Then also was the New Covenant sealed, and the heirs of the eternal kingdom were inscribed with the blood of Christ. Then was evidently effected the transition from the Law to the Gospel, from the Synagogue to the Church, from the many legal sacrifices to the one Sacrifice, in such a manner that, when the Lord gave up His spirit, the mystical veil which concealed the innermost part of the Temple and its holy mystery from view was suddenly and violently rent in twain from top to bottom.

"Then truth abolished the figures ... and the prophecies became superfluous after their fulfilment.

"The tearing asunder of the veil before the entrance to the Holy of Holies of the Old Dispensation was a sign that the Old Covenant ceased when the New and eternal Covenant of grace had been instituted in the blood of Christ. With the ending of the Old Covenant, the ancient sacrifices also ceased, because they had become useless."

Ibid., pp. 79, 80.

b. "The Church of Christ is placed in the middle between the figurative shadow of the Old Law and the final completion of the Heavenly Jerusalem.

"The Old Dispensation was the preparation and the breaking of the ground for Christianity; and Christianity forms the direct entrance and vestibule leading to the revealed and beatific vision of the eternal truth and beauty to come. But the perfection of religion necessarily demands a perfect divine worship, that is, the offering of sacrifice; for sacrifice is the chief and most excellent act of religion."

Ibid., p. 81.

6. The Eucharistic Sacrifice

a. "Grace does not destroy nature, but improves and sanctifies, ennobles and transforms it; hence man requires, . . . a visible sacrifice in order to comply with his religious obligations in a manner most consonant with his nature.

" 'Human nature,' as the Church says, 'requires a visible sacrifice'; hence God, whose providence arranges all things . . . would assuredly not leave Christians without a permanent sacrifice which so greatly accords with the inmost wants of a religious heart."

Ibid., p. 80.

b. "By the New Law Christ did not abolish the imperfect sacrificial worship of the Old Law, but changed it into one . . . more perfect."

Ibid., p. 81.

c. "The Last Supper was not merely a communion celebration, but also a sacrificial celebration; for 'after partaking of the figurative lamb,' our Lord, by His creative omnipotent word, changed the earthly elements of bread and wine into His holy Body and divine Blood, that is, He placed His Body and His Blood in the sacramental state of sacrifice, offered Himself thus to His Father and then gave His Body and His Blood offered in sacrifice to His disciples as food and drink."

Ibid., p. 93.

d. "Jesus Christ Himself offered the first Eucharistic Sacrifice in the Supper Room of Jerusalem, and this in close connection with the eating of the Paschal Lamb of the Old Testament."

Ibid., p. 331.

e. "St. Luke gives the words of consecration thus: 'This is the chalice, the new testament of My blood, which [chalice] shall be shed for you'; St. Matthew: 'For this is My blood of the new testament, which shall be shed for many, unto the remission of sins.' Vicariously to shed blood for the atonement of the sins of others is an expression frequently employed in Holy Writ to designate sacrifice. Hence the words of the institution convey this idea: This is the chalice which is offered for you; this is My blood which is offered for many, in order to blot out sins. Our Lord, therefore, declares that He presents His sacrificial blood to His disciples as drink, and that His blood is offered in sacrifice. The words of our Lord are (according to the original Greek text) so constituted that they directly and expressly designate the offering of His blood by a mystical or mysterious shedding in the chalice, and not that of a true and real shedding of His blood on the Cross."

Ibid., p. 93.

f. "Our Saviour named His blood, contained and shed in the chalice, the 'blood of the New Testament' (Matthew 26:28). The word testament has here a twofold meaning; namely, covenant and legacy. Christ is the mediator of a better covenant, which is established on better promises (Hebrews 8:6) and that is the new covenant of grace."

Ibid., p. 96.

g. "The Eucharistic Blood, which flowed in the chalice for the sealing of the new covenant, was the sacrificial blood of Jesus Christ shed for the glory of God. This celebration of the Eucharist established by our Lord became, consequently, a true and real sacrifice."

Ibid., p. 97.

h. "But the blood only cannot be shed, that is, sacrificed, without the body being, at the same time, also sacrificed; body and blood constitute together but one sacrificial gift. . . .

"According to St. Luke our Lord consecrated the bread with the words: 'This is My body which is given for you. . . .' "

Ibid., p. 94.

i. "Christ before His death not only offered Himself in an unbloody manner, but He moreover instituted a perpetual unbloody Sacrifice. This is easily proved. In the following words: 'Do this for a commemoration of Me' (*Hoc facite in meam commemorationem* — Luke 22:19), the Lord commanded His Apostles and their successors in the priestly dignity (1 Cor. 2:24-27) to do the same (*hoc*) as He had done, until His return at the end of time; that is, continually to offer the Eucharistic Sacrifice, which He had just offered in their presence. By this command, as a natural consequence, He also imparted to them the power of consecration, or of offering sacrifice, that is, He made them priests of the New Law. Thus our Lord instituted the Eucharistic Sacrifice, and willed to transmit the power to offer it to priests only, to whom it appertains to partake of it and to distribute it to the rest."

Ibid., pp. 95, 96.

j. "The doctrine and practice of the Apostles prove that they henceforth celebrated the Eucharist as the Sacrifice of the Christian religion."

Ibid., p. 98.

k. "Upon earth also does our glorified Saviour continually exercise His office of Highpriest — and that by the accomplishment of a true and real sacrifice; for He is the chief Sacrificial Priest, Who upon the altar, by the hands of His duly authorized ministers, ever performs the Eucharistic actions of sacrifice."

Ibid., p. 78.

l. "At the altar, the officiating priest acts not merely as the representative and as the organ of Christ, but also in the name and under the
authority of the Church. For the Eucharist is the property of the
Catholic Church: to her our Lord bequeathed the Eucharistic Sacrifice,
that she might always be able to render to the Most High due honor
and glory, as well as to dispense with lavish hand to her needy children the fulness and riches of all blessings."
                                                     Ibid., p. 118.

m. "The priest . . . celebrates in the name of the Church, in the name of
the whole Christian people, so that in as far as they are members of
the Church, all the faithful at least habitually offer through him as
their representative the Eucharistic Sacrifice. For this reason also the
Prince of the Apostles calls all Christians 'a holy and a kingly priesthood' (1 Peter 2:5-9), that is, called 'to offer up spiritual sacrifices,
acceptable to God through Jesus Christ.'"
                                                     Ibid., p. 119.

n. "As the Eternal Highpriest according to the order of Melchisedech,
Christ does not and will not cease until the consummation of time to
offer Himself in the Mass to His heavenly Father; but now He no
longer does so alone in a personal, visible manner, as He did at the
Last Supper and upon the Cross, but invisibly and with the assistance
of a human representative."
                                                     Ibid., p. 117.

o. "The priest at the altar is the representative and image of the praying
and sacrificing Saviour. . . ."
                                                     Ibid., p. 584.

p. "Although Christ's precious Blood, which is mystically shed in the
chalice, has an infinite, eternal and imperishable value, nevertheless,
this of itself, would not suffice to impart infinite value to the Eucharistic Sacrifice, since, for this purpose it is requisite, above all, that
the Person Who celebrates should possess infinite greatness and majesty, as is the case with the God-Man and with Him alone."
                                                     Ibid., p. 136.

q. "The Eucharistic Sacrificial action consists in the double consecration,
by which the body and blood of Christ, under the appearances of bread
and wine, are placed in a state of sacrifice and are, therefore, sacrificed.
All the prayers, ceremonies and actions that partly precede and partly
follow the consecration in the celebration of the Mass are, consequently, not essential to the Eucharistic Sacrifice."
                                                     Ibid., p. 120.

r. "The complete essence of the Eucharistic Sacrifice consists, therefore,
in the mystical shedding of blood wrought by the words consecrating

both elements; and, indeed, it consists in this blood-shedding, inasmuch as said blood-shedding is a real expression of the present intention of sacrifice and of the self-offering of Christ taking place on the altar, and, at the same time, in so far as it represents and renews the Sacrifice of the Cross."

Ibid., p. 123.

s. "The Sacrifice of the Cross, therefore, was infinitely painful. Here on our altar His human nature is glorified and immortal — the Sacrifice of the Mass, consequently, is a sacrifice free from pain. The object of the Sacrifice of the Cross was to obtain the price of the redemption of the world; the purpose of the Sacrifice of the Mass is to apply to individual man the treasures of grace merited and amassed by the Sacrifice of the Cross."

Ibid., p. 130.

t. "As 'the pillar and ground of the truth' (1 Timothy 3:15), the Catholic Church has always and everywhere believed and taught that the Holy Mass is a true Sacrifice — the sole and perpetual Sacrifice of the New Law."

Ibid., p. 100.

u. "Christ has placed Himself in the hands of the Church, that she may offer Him to the heavenly Father; with the infinitely meritorious and acceptable sacrifice to God of the body and blood of Christ, the Church unites the offering of herself. In union with the sacrifice of Christ, the faithful should offer themselves with all their labors, sufferings and prayers with body and soul."

Ibid., p. 131.

v. " 'Principally' and 'in the first place' (*imprimis*) the Eucharistic Sacrifice is offered for the 'Holy Catholic Church of God' (*pro Ecclesia tua sancta catholica*) ; hence from every Mass there flows to her abundant fruits and blessings."

Ibid., p. 593.

w. "THE CELEBRATION OF HOLY MASS IS THE MOST WORTHY AND THE MOST PERFECT DIVINE SERVICE; FOR IT PROCURES TO THE MOST HIGH A WORSHIP AND A VENERATION WHICH MILLIONS OF WORLDS WOULD BE INCAPABLE OF RENDERING HIM. THE EUCHARISTIC SACRIFICE IS OF ITSELF THE MOST GLORIOUS CHANT TO THE PRAISE AND GLORY OF THE TRIUNE GOD. IT IS THE SUMMARY OF DIVINE WORSHIP; FOR IT IS OUR HIGHEST ADORATION AND BEST THANKSGIVING, OUR MOST EFFICACIOUS PROPITIATION AND MOST POWERFUL PETITION."

Ibid., p. 197.

7. "Missa"

a. "Since the mind of man is too limited and his language too feeble to express perfectly the Mystery of the Eucharistic Sacrifice, there have been even from the most ancient times a number of titles bestowed upon it, each of which, however, brings into prominence but some one side of the Mystery; yet not one of them exhausts its unfathomably deep and rich contents.

"Among these names that of *Missa* (Mass) deserves a more particular explanation, as it is almost the only one employed since the early part of the middle ages to designate the Eucharistic Sacrifice.

"The word 'Missa' (*Missio,* i. e., *dimissio*) denotes the solemn dismissal or departure of those present after the conclusion of divine service; this signification it even now retains in the well-known concluding formula given: 'Ite, missa est' — 'Go, it is the dismissal.' . . . "

Ibid., pp. 328, 329.

b. "The name *Missa* which in the beginning, . . . signified the dismissal from divine service of persons assisting thereat, was thus transferred to the celebration of divine worship itself."

Ibid., p. 330.

8. The Canon of the Mass

a. "THE CANON OF THE MASS, which begins after the *SANCTUS* and ends before the *PATER NOSTER* includes the Consecration, or Sacrificial Act, as also those prayers and ceremonies that introduce the Consecration and are most closely connected with it. It therefore covers the divine sacrificial act with a mystical veil and encloses it in a more precious case.

"As the Sacrifice which the eternal Highpriest offers on the altar to the end of ages, is and ever remains the same, so in like manner the Canon, the ecclesiastical sacrificial prayer, in its sublime simplicity and venerable majesty, is and ever remains invariably the same; only on the greatest feasts are a few additions made in order to harmonize with the spirit and change of the ecclesiastical year."

Ibid., p. 579.

b. "WITH THE CANON OF CONSECRATION ARE USHERED IN THE HOLIEST AND MOST SACRED MOMENTS OF THE SAC-RIFICIAL CELEBRATION: THIS PART OF HOLY MASS, STILL MORE THAN THE OTHER PORTIONS, CLAIMS ATTENTION, DEVOTION AND REVERENCE."

Ibid., p. 585.

c. "The moment of the Consecration is the moment the most important and solemn, the most sublime and touching, the most holy and fruitful of the whole sacrificial celebration; for it includes that glorious and unfathomably profound work, namely, the accomplishment of the Eucharistic Sacrifice, in which all the marvels of God's love are concentrated as in a focus of heat and light."

Ibid., p. 632.

d. "That the God-Man did shed His blood for us on the Cross, and that He again sheds it for us in a mystical manner on the altar — is an adorable divine achievement which includes in itself the sum of the most unheard-of wonders, all of which can be acknowledged and believed as true only in the light and the power of faith. Christ's sacrificial blood in the chalice is a mystery of faith in the fullest sense of the term."

Ibid., p. 641.

e. "The twofold Consecration is a mystical shedding of blood, and places before our eyes in a most lively manner the bloody death of Christ sacrificed on the Cross.

"The Sacrifice on the altar is indeed painless; for the Saviour is no longer passible and can no longer suffer death. But His divinely human Heart is here inflamed with the same love of sacrifice, and is moved by the same obedience to His Father to sacrifice Himself as when He was on the Cross. This love and this obedience urged Him to sacrifice Himself mystically on the altar also under the twofold sacramental appearances.

"IT IS AT THE MOMENT OF CONSECRATION THAT THE SACRIFICE IS ACCOMPLISHED, IS OFFERED TO GOD AND PLACED IN THE HANDS OF US POOR MORTALS. . . . For the senses alone nothing has happened, nothing is changed; for the appearances of bread and wine, upheld by the power of God, have remained to serve as veil and covering for the bright majesty of the King of Glory, Who with us and for us is present as Victim on the altar. . . .

"Truly, no moment commands greater reverence, no moment is more holy or more beneficial than that in which the Eucharistic Sacrifice is accomplished and the altar becomes a mystical Mount Calvary."

Ibid., pp. 641, 642.

f. "As once on Mount Calvary, so Christ, here on the altar, as the great Mediator, as the true Victim and as the Eternal Highpriest, is elevated betwixt heaven and earth, to reconcile God and man, inasmuch as He moves the heavenly Father to mercy and forgiveness and rouses sinful man to love and compunction."

Ibid., p. 645.

g. "At the moment of Consecration Jesus Christ as Highpriest offers Himself up through the Holy Ghost and the ministry of the visible priest to the honor of His heavenly Father, as well as for our salvation. AND AT THE SAME TIME HE PLACES HIS SACRIFICIAL BODY AND SACRIFICIAL BLOOD IN THE HANDS OF THE CHURCH.

"The Church now presents to the majesty of the Father, as her Sacrifice, the Victim mystically immolated, whilst including the sacrifice of her own self as a gift in union with the infinitely meritorious sacrificial body and sacrificial blood of Christ."

Ibid., p. 656.

h. "THE HOST IS BROKEN IN ORDER MORE VIVIDLY TO REPRESENT IN A LITURGICAL MANNER THE EUCHARIST'S CHARACTER AS A SACRIFICE; for the breaking symbolizes in an expressive way Christ's violent and bloody death on the Cross, inasmuch as it indicates that wounding and lacerating which caused the separation of His soul from His body, . . . and resulted in His death. In the fraction of the Host, Christ is figured as the Lamb that was slain and bruised for our sins (Isaias 53:5)."

Ibid., p. 705.

9. The Communion of the Mass

a. ". . . To eat the flesh of Christ is the same thing as to be incorporated into the Church, to be aggregated and associated to it, and so to be brought into Christ and to drink and participate in His Spirit.

". . . It may be added that the Eucharist is not only a symbol, but a cause of this union of the faithful in the Church. For as out of many grains of wheat ground together one loaf is made, and out of many clusters of grapes pressed together wine floweth, so of many faithful communicants is one society and Church."

Cornelius à Lapide (St. John 6:52).

b. "I reply, therefore, (1) that as regards the thing (*rem*) contained in the Sacrament, THE LAITY DO ALSO DRINK THE BLOOD OF CHRIST WHEN THEY RECEIVE HIS BODY UNDER THE SPECIES OF BREAD. Because under that species, by virtue of consecration, there is there the body of Christ, but by concomitance there is under the same the blood of Christ, for the body of Christ is not bloodless, nor can the blood of Christ be separated from His glorified body.

"As therefore he who takes the Eucharist under the species of wine by virtue of the words of consecration, takes directly and primarily the blood of Christ, and yet by concomitance takes the body of Christ, because the blood of Christ cannot be without His flesh; so in turn he who takes the flesh of Christ under the species of bread, takes directly the flesh of Christ, but by concomitance takes also His blood."

Ibid. (St. John 6:54).

c. "And the expression of St. Paul, 'the body broken for you' (*corpus pro vobis fractum*), is of such a nature that it unequivocally designates the Sacrifice of the Eucharist. The word 'broken' (*frangere*) can in this place be applied only to the body of Christ, inasmuch as, under the appearance of bread, it is presented and eaten as a food; for only the Eucharistic Body is broken or distributed.

"The literal meaning of the Apostle is, therefore: This is my body which as food under the appearance of bread is broken for you. Now, these words necessarily have the same meaning as those of St. Luke: 'This is My body which is given for you,' that is, sacrificed; hence they must in like manner express the Sacrifice of the body of Christ.

"The full meaning of the words of St. Paul is accordingly: This is My body which is sacrificed for you in the sacramental state, in which it is given as food. Thus Christ gave His body primarily to His heavenly Father as a sacrifice for His disciples; and He then distributed to them His body sacrificed for them to be eaten as food. By this He accomplished a former prediction: 'The bread [of heaven] that I will give is My flesh for the life of the world' [*pro mundi vita*] (John 6:52)."

Gihr, op. cit., pp. 95, 96.

10.   With Christ, in Christ, through Christ

a. "With Christ, in Christ and through Christ, the Church during Mass daily offers herself to the Most High 'as a holy living sacrifice, pleasing unto God' (Romans 12:1).

"*With Christ:* At the sight of the Divine Victim, Whose body is daily mystically broken upon the altar and Whose blood is daily mystically shed before our eyes, she is encouraged and animated cheerfully to drink with Him of the chalice of bitter affliction, to embrace with joy labors and sufferings, persecutions and calumnies.

"*In Christ:* For in Him as her Head, that is, in her most intimate connection and fusion with His Sacrifice, the Church offers herself to tread the rough and lonely, the weary and painful way of the Cross, until she shall have arrived at the heavenly Jerusalem.

"*Through Christ:* For the true and mystical body of Christ (*corpus verum et mysticum*) constitutes the sole sacrifice, whose sweet odor ascends to heaven, 'through Christ our Lord,' through Whom alone we may approach to God, and by Whom alone we can please Him."

Ibid., p. 132.

b. "Christ redeemed the world, as Supreme Teacher, inasmuch as He announced the truths of faith; as Highpriest, inasmuch as He established peace between heaven and earth and regained for us the gifts of
grace; as Divine King, inasmuch as He founded a kingdom which,
although in this world, is not of this world — a supernatural kingdom
of truth, of grace and of love, wherein He reigns over hearts. Christ
continues to exercise His office of Teacher, of Priest and of Shepherd
over the whole world in the Holy Sacrifice of the Mass."

Ibid., p. 193.

11. Liturgy

a. "Christ Himself instituted and ordained merely the essential sacrificial act; but all that appertains to the liturgical development, representation and investment of the divine sacrificial act He left to His
Church, directed and enlightened by the Holy Ghost."

Ibid., p. 229.

b. "The Eucharistic Sacrifice is therefore the soul or life of the entire
divine worship, the sun that illumines all religious celebrations, the
heart that gives pulse to all sacramental cult, the fountain-head of the
whole ecclesiastical life of grace. IN SHORT, IT IS THE CENTER
OF THE CATHOLIC LITURGY."

Ibid., p. 206.

c. "That overruling influence of the Spirit of God that directs, even in
secondary matters, the affairs of the visible Church, nowhere else appears so marked and evident as in the arrangement of the rite of the
Holy Mass, which . . . in its present state forms such a beautiful, perfect
whole, yea, a splendid work, that it excites the admiration of every re-
flecting mind."

Ibid., p. 337.

d. "The chalice and the paten occupy the first place of honor among the
sacred vessels; for in the chalice the infinitely precious blood of Christ
is consecrated, and on the paten the glorious body of the Lord is
placed."

Ibid., p. 258.

e. "Our Missal is principally derived from the Sacramentary of St.
Gregory the Great. Under him the Canon of the Mass received its last
addition. The rest of the constituent parts of the Roman liturgy of
the Mass (the *Introit*, the *Kyrie*, the *Gloria*, the *Collect*, the *Epistle*,
the *Gradual*, the *Gospel*, the *Secreta*, the *Preface*, the *Pater Noster*,
the *Communion* and the *Post Communion*) date back at least to the
fifth or even the fourth century."

Ibid., p. 336.

F.   BIBLICAL BACKGROUND

A principle deeply involved in the Protestant revolt of the sixteenth century was that of private interpretation of the Bible.

This is why the teaching concerning the Infallibility of the Church should be thoroughly understood by the teacher as a background in giving the First Communion lessons and for direct training of children in the fifth grade and beyond.

Upon this basis several Sovereign Pontiffs have written letters recommending the reading of Holy Scripture by the laity.

Pope Leo XIII, in his encyclical on the study of Holy Scripture, "Providentissimus Deus," says:

"Let all, therefore, especially the novices of the ecclesiastical army, understand how deeply the Sacred Books should be esteemed, and with what eagerness and reverence they should approach this great arsenal of heavenly arms. For those whose duty it is to handle Catholic doctrine before the learned or unlearned will nowhere find more ample matter or more abundant exhortation."

The following Scripture texts will surely give vitality to the teacher's presentation of Holy Church and Holy Mass.

Jesus' Church

1.   God's Holy Church and His Priesthood: The Old Law

a. Deuteronomy 17:8, 9

"If thou perceive that there be among you a hard and doubtful matter in judgment between blood and blood, . . . arise and go up to the place which the Lord thy God shall choose. And thou shalt come to the priests of the Levitical race. . . . "

b. 2 Paralipomenon 6:18-21

"Is it credible then that God should dwell with men on the earth? If heaven, and the heavens of heavens, do not contain Thee, how much less this house which I have built?

"But to this end only it is made, that Thou mayest regard the prayer of Thy servant and his supplication, O Lord my God; and mayest hear the prayers which Thy servant poureth out before Thee.

"That Thou mayest open Thy eyes upon this house day and night, upon the place wherein Thou hast promised that Thy name should be called upon.

"And that Thou wouldst hear the prayer which Thy servant prayeth in it hearken then to the prayers of Thy servant, and of Thy people Israel. Whosoever shall pray in this place, hear Thou from Thy dwelling place, that is, from heaven, and show mercy."

c. Psalm 22:1-3

"The Lord ruleth me: and I shall want nothing. He hath set me in a place of pasture. . . . He hath led me on the paths of justice, for His own name's sake."

Psalm 45:5, 6

"The stream of the river maketh the city of God joyful: the Most High hath sanctified His own tabernacle. God is in the midst thereof, it shall not be moved: God will help it in the morning early."

Psalm 78:13

"But we Thy people and the sheep of Thy pasture, will give thanks to Thee forever. . . ."

Psalm 95:6-9

"Praise and beauty are before Him: holiness and majesty in His SANCTUARY. . . . Adore ye the Lord in His holy court. Let all the earth be moved at His presence."

Psalm 117:22

"The stone which the builders rejected; the same is become the head of the corner."

d. Isaias 2:2, 3

"And in the last days the mountain of the house of the Lord shall be prepared on the top of the mountains, and it shall be exalted above the hills and all nations shall flow unto it, and many people shall go; . . . and He will teach us His ways and we will walk in His paths. . . ."

Isaias 28:16

"Behold I will lay a stone in the foundations of Sion, a tried stone, a corner stone. . . ."

Isaias 35:8
"And a path and a way shall be there, and it shall be called the holy way: . . . and this shall be unto you a straight way, so that fools shall not err therein."

Isaias 40:11
"He shall feed His flock like a shepherd: He shall gather together the lambs with His arm. . . . "

Isaias 59:20, 21
"And there shall come a Redeemer to Sion. . . . This is My covenant with them. . . . My spirit that is in thee and my words that I have put in thy mouth shall not depart out of thy mouth . . . from henceforth and forever."

e. Ezechiel 34:15
"I will feed My sheep: and I will cause them to lie down, saith the Lord God."

Ezechiel 34:23
"AND I WILL SET UP ONE SHEPHERD OVER THEM and he shall feed them, even my servant David; he shall feed them, and he shall be their shepherd."

Ezechiel 37:24, 26, 27
" . . . AND THEY SHALL HAVE ONE SHEPHERD. . . . I will establish them, and will set My sanctuary in the midst of them forever, and My tabernacle shall be with them. . . . "

Ezechiel 37:28
"And the nations shall know that I am the Lord, the Sanctifier of Israel, when My sanctuary shall be in the midst of them forever."

f. Daniel 2:44
" . . . The God of heaven will set up a kingdom that shall never be destroyed, and His kingdom shall not be delivered up to another people and it shall break in pieces, and shall consume all these kingdoms, and itself shall stand forever."

Daniel 7:14
" . . . His power is an everlasting power, that shall not be taken away: and His kingdom that shall not be destroyed."

g. Micheas 4:1, 2

"And it shall come to pass in the last days, that the mountain of the house of the Lord shall be prepared in the top of mountains, and high above the hills: and people shall flow to it.... And many nations shall come in haste ... and He will teach us of His ways...."

h. Aggeus 2:8, 10

"And I will move all nations: AND THE DESIRED OF ALL NATIONS SHALL COME: and I will fill this house with glory, saith the Lord of hosts.... Great shall be the glory of this last house, more than of the first, saith the Lord of hosts: and in this place I will give peace, saith the Lord of hosts."

i. Zacharias 8:3

"Thus saith the Lord of hosts: I am returned to Sion, and I will dwell in the midst of Jerusalem: and Jerusalem shall be called the City of Truth, and the Mountains of the Lord of Hosts, the sanctified Mountains."

j. Apocalypse 21:3

"And I heard a great voice from the throne saying: Behold the tabernacle of God with men, and He will dwell with them. And they shall be His people: and God Himself with them shall be their God."

2. Jesus, "the Son of the Living God"

a. Matthew 3:17

"And behold a voice from heaven saying: THIS IS MY BELOVED SON, in Whom I am well pleased."
(See Matthew 17:5; Luke 9:35; 2 Peter 1:17)

Matthew 8:28, 29

"... And behold, they [the devils] cried out, saying: What have we to do with Thee, JESUS, SON OF GOD?..."

Matthew 14:32, 33

"... And they that were in the boat came and adored Him saying: Indeed THOU ART THE SON OF GOD."

Matthew 16:13, 16

"... Simon Peter answered and said: THOU ART CHRIST, THE SON OF THE LIVING GOD."
(See John 6:68-70)

Matthew 27:43

"... For He said: I AM THE SON OF GOD."

Matthew 27:54

"Now the centurion and they that were with him watching Jesus, having seen the earthquake, and the things that were done, were sore afraid, saying: INDEED THIS WAS THE SON OF GOD."

b. ### Mark 1:23, 24

"... What have we [a man with an unclean spirit] to do with Thee, Jesus of Nazareth? Art Thou come to destroy us? I know Who Thou art, THE HOLY ONE OF GOD."

Mark 3:11, 12

"... And they [the unclean spirits], when they saw Him, fell down before Him: and they cried saying: THOU ART THE SON OF GOD...."

Mark 5:2-7

"... And crying with a loud voice, he [a man with an unclean spirit] said: What have I to do with Thee, JESUS, THE SON OF THE MOST HIGH GOD?..."

Mark 14:61, 62

"And again the highpriest asked Him, and said to Him: ART THOU THE CHRIST, THE SON OF THE BLESSED GOD?... AND JESUS SAID TO HIM: I AM...."

c. ### Luke 1:30-35

"... And therefore also the Holy which shall be born of thee shall be called THE SON OF GOD."

Luke 4:41

"And devils went out from many, crying out and saying: THOU ART THE SON OF GOD...."

Luke 22:70, 71

"Then said they all: ART THOU THEN THE SON OF GOD? Who said: You say that I am. And they said: WHAT NEED WE ANY FURTHER TESTIMONY? FOR WE OURSELVES HAVE HEARD IT FROM HIS OWN MOUTH."

d. ### John 1:14

"And the Word was made flesh, and dwelt among us (and we saw His glory, the glory as it were of THE ONLY-BEGOTTEN OF THE FATHER)...."

John 1:29-34
"The next day, John saw Jesus coming to him, and he saith: Behold the Lamb of God. ... And I saw, and I gave testimony, that THIS IS THE SON OF GOD."

John 11:25-27
" ... She [Martha] saith to Him: Yea, Lord, I HAVE BELIEVED THAT THOU ART CHRIST THE SON OF THE LIVING GOD, Who art come into this world."

John 20:30, 31
"Many other signs also did Jesus in the sight of His disciples, which are not written in this book. But these are written, that you may believe that JESUS IS THE CHRIST, THE SON OF GOD: and that believing you may have life in His name."

e. Acts 18:28
"For with much vigor he [Apollo] convinced the Jews openly, showing by the Scriptures that JESUS IS THE CHRIST."

3. Jesus, "the Head of the Corner"

a. Matthew 21:42
"Jesus saith to them: Have you never read in the Scriptures: The stone which the builders rejected, the same is become the head of the corner? By the Lord this has been done; ... "
(See Luke 20:17)

b. Acts 4:10, 11
"Be it known to you all, and to all the people of Israel, that by the name of our Lord Jesus Christ of Nazareth, Whom you crucified, Whom God hath raised from the dead, even by Him, this man standeth here before you whole. This is the stone which was rejected by you the builders, which is become the head of the corner."

c. Ephesians 2:19-21
" ... Built upon the foundation of the Apostles and Prophets, Jesus Christ Himself being the chief corner stone. In Whom all the building, being framed together, growing up into an holy temple in the Lord."

d. I Peter 2:4, 6, 7
"Unto Whom coming, as to a living stone, rejected indeed by men, but chosen and made honorable by God. ... Behold I lay in Sion a chief corner stone, ... the stone which the builders rejected. ... "

4. Jesus, "the Way, the Truth and the Life"

a. John 1:4

"In Him was LIFE, and the LIFE was the light of men."

John 6:40

"And this is the will of My Father that sent Me: that everyone who seeth the Son, and believeth in Him, may have LIFE EVERLAST-ING, and I will raise him up in the last day."

John 8:12

"... Jesus spoke to them saying: I am THE LIGHT OF THE WORLD: HE THAT FOLLOWETH ME, walketh not in darkness but SHALL HAVE THE LIGHT OF LIFE."

John 11:25

"Jesus said: ... I am the resurrection AND THE LIFE: he that believeth in Me, although he be dead, SHALL LIVE. And everyone that liveth, and believeth in Me, SHALL NOT DIE FOREVER."

John 14:6

"Jesus saith: I AM THE WAY, AND THE TRUTH, AND THE LIFE. No man cometh to the Father but by me."

b. Acts 13:47

"For so the Lord hath commanded us: I have set thee to be THE LIGHT OF THE GENTILES; that thou mayest be for salvation unto the utmost part of the earth."
(See Isaias 42:6 and 49:6)

c. Colossians 3:4

"When Christ shall appear WHO IS YOUR LIFE, you also shall appear with Him in glory."

d. I John 5:11, 12

"And this is the testimony, that God hath given us eternal life. AND THIS LIFE IS IN HIS SON. HE THAT HATH THE SON, HATH LIFE. He that hath not the Son, hath not life."

I John 5:20

"And we know that the Son of God is come: and He hath given us understanding THAT WE MAY KNOW THE TRUE GOD, AND MAY BE IN HIS TRUE SON. THIS IS THE TRUE GOD AND LIFE ETERNAL."

5. Jesus' Holy Church and His Priesthood: the New Law

a. Matthew 10:1-8
Jesus chooses His Apostles.

Matthew 10:40
"He that receiveth you, receiveth Me: and he that receiveth Me, receiveth Him that sent Me."

Matthew 16:18, 19
"AND I SAY TO THEE: THAT THOU ART PETER, AND UPON THIS ROCK I WILL BUILD MY CHURCH, AND THE GATES OF HELL SHALL NOT PREVAIL AGAINST IT. AND I WILL GIVE TO THEE THE KEYS OF THE KINGDOM OF HEAVEN. ..."

Matthew 18:17
"And if he will not hear them, tell the Church. And if he will not hear the Church, let him be to thee as the heathen and publican."

Matthew 28:18-20
"And Jesus coming, spoke to them, saying: All power is given to Me in heaven and in earth. Going therefore teach ye all nations. ... AND BEHOLD, I AM WITH YOU ALL DAYS, EVEN TO THE CONSUMMATION OF THE WORLD."

b. Luke 6:12-17
Jesus chooses His Apostles.

Luke 10:16
"He that heareth you, heareth Me; and he that despiseth you, despiseth Me, and he that despiseth Me, despiseth Him that sent Me."

Luke 22:31, 32
"... Simon, Simon, behold Satan hath desired to have you, that he may sift you as wheat: BUT I HAVE PRAYED FOR THEE, THAT THY FAITH FAIL NOT: and thou, being converted, confirm thy brethren."

c. John 10:9-15
"I am the door. By Me if any man enter in, he shall be saved: and he shall go in, and go out, and shall find pastures. ... I am the Good Shepherd. The Good Shepherd giveth His life for His sheep: I am the Good Shepherd. ..."

John 13:20

" . . . He that receiveth whomsoever I send, receiveth Me. . . . "

John 14:16, 17, 26

"And I will ask the Father, and He shall give you another Paraclete, that He may abide with you forever. The spirit of Truth. . . . But the Paraclete, the Holy Ghost Whom the Father will send in My name, He will teach you all things. . . . "

John 15:5-8

"I am the vine; you the branches: he that abideth in Me, and I in him, the same beareth much fruit: for without Me you can do nothing."

John 16:13

"But when He, the Spirit of Truth, is come, He will teach you all truth. . . . "

John 17:18

"As Thou hast sent Me into the world, I also have sent them into the world."

John 18:37

" . . . FOR THIS WAS I BORN, AND FOR THIS CAME I INTO THE WORLD; THAT I SHOULD GIVE TESTIMONY TO THE TRUTH. EVERYONE THAT IS OF THE TRUTH, HEARETH MY VOICE."

John 20:21

"He said therefore to them again: Peace be to you. AS THE FATHER HATH SENT ME, I ALSO SEND YOU."

John 21:15-17

"Jesus saith to Simon Peter: Simon, son of John, lovest thou Me more than these? . . . Feed My lambs. . . . Feed My sheep. . . . "

d. Acts 1:8

" . . . But you shall receive the power of the Holy Ghost, . . . and you shall be witnesses unto Me in Jerusalem, and in all Judea, and Samaria, and even to the uttermost part of the earth."

Acts 6:6

"These they set before the Apostles; and they praying, IMPOSED HANDS upon them."

Acts 13:3

"Then they, fasting and praying, AND IMPOSING THEIR HANDS UPON THEM [Saul and Barnabas], sent them away."

Acts 14:22

"And when they had ordained to them priests in every church. . . . "

Acts 16:4, 5

"And as they [Paul and Silas] passed through the cities, they delivered unto them the decrees for to keep, that were decreed by the Apostles and ancients who were at Jerusalem. And the churches were confirmed in faith and increased in number daily."

Acts 20:28

"Take heed to yourselves, and to the whole flock wherein the Holy Ghost hath placed you bishops to rule the Church of God, which He hath purchased with His own blood."

e. I Timothy 2:3-8

"For this is good and acceptable in the sight of God our Saviour. . . . Whereunto I am appointed a preacher and an Apostle (I say the truth, I lie not), a doctor of the Gentiles in faith and truth."

I Timothy 3:15

". . . WHICH IS THE CHURCH OF THE LIVING GOD, THE PILLAR AND GROUND OF TRUTH."

f. 2 Timothy 1:6

"For which cause I admonish thee, that thou stir up the grace of God which is in thee, by the imposition of my hands."

g. Titus 1:5

"For this cause I left thee in Crete, that thou shouldst . . . ordain priests in every city, as I also appointed thee."

h. Hebrews 13:7-17

"Remember your prelates who have spoken the word of God to you. . . . Obey your prelates, and be subject to them. . . . "

i. I Peter 2:25

"For you were as sheep going astray; but you are now converted to the shepherd and bishop of your souls."

j. I John 4:6

"We are of God. He that knoweth God heareth us. He that is not of God, heareth us not. By this we know the Spirit of truth and the spirit of error."

6. Jesus, Head of the Mystical Body

a. Romans 12:4, 5

"For as in one body we have many members, but all the members have not the same office: so we, being many, are one body in Christ, and everyone members one of another."

b. I Corinthians 12:12

"For as the body is one, and hath many members; and all the members of the body, whereas they are many, YET ARE ONE BODY, SO, ALSO IS CHRIST."

I Corinthians 12:26, 27

"And if one member suffer anything, all the members suffer with it; or if one member glory, all the members rejoice with it. NOW YOU ARE THE BODY OF CHRIST, AND MEMBERS OF MEMBER."

c. Ephesians 1:22, 23

"And He hath subjected all things under His feet, and HATH MADE HIM HEAD OVER ALL THE CHURCH. WHICH IS HIS BODY...."

Ephesians 4:11-15

"And he gave some Apostles, and some Prophets, and other some Evangelists, and other some pastors and doctors. For ... the edifying of the body of Christ.... That henceforth we be no more children tossed to and fro and carried about with every wind of doctrine by the wickedness of men, by cunning craftiness by which they lie in wait to deceive us. But doing the truth in charity, we may in all things grow up in Him Who is the Head, even Christ."

Ephesians 5:23-30

"The husband is the head of the wife as Christ is the head of the Church. Therefore, as the Church is subject to Christ, so also, let the wives be to their husbands. Husbands, love your wives, as Christ also loved the Church, and delivered Himself up for it.... That He might present it to Himself a glorious Church, not having spot or wrinkle, or any such thing; but that it should be holy and without blemish.... For no man ever hateth his own flesh; but nourisheth and cherisheth it, as also Christ doth the Church: because we are members of His body."

d. Colossians 1:18

"And He is the head of the body of the Church ... THAT IN ALL THINGS HE MAY HOLD THE PRIMACY."

The Holy Sacrifice of the Mass

Texts pertaining to the Feast of the Passover and to the offering of sacrifices according to the Old Law are essential to the teacher's background in understanding and teaching "The Holy Sacrifice of the Mass," although in the series, "A Little Child's First Communion," "The Offering of Sacrifices according to the Old Law" is not presented to the child.

1. The Priesthood and the Offering of Sacrifices according to the Old Law

a. Genesis 4:3-6

"... Cain offered of the fruits of the earth, gifts to the Lord. Abel also offered of the firstlings of his flock, and of their fat: and the Lord had respect to Abel, and to his offerings. But. . . . "
(See Hebrews 11:4)

Genesis 8:20

"And Noe built an altar unto the Lord: . . . and offered holocausts upon the altar. And the Lord . . . said: I will no more curse the earth for the sake of man. . . . "

Genesis 14:18, 19

"But MELCHISEDECH, the king of Salem, BRINGING FORTH BREAD AND WINE, for he was the priest of the most high God; blessed him [Abraham] and said: Blessed be Abraham by the most high God. . . . "
(See Hebrews, chapter 7)

Genesis 22:2-13

"He [God] said to him [Abraham]: Take thy only-begotten son Isaac, whom thou lovest, and go into the land of vision: and there THOU SHALT OFFER HIM FOR AN HOLOCAUST upon one of the mountains which I shall show you. . . .

"Now I know that thou fearest God, and hast not spared thy only-begotten son for My sake."

b. Exodus 12:21-24

"And Moses called all the ancients of the children of Israel, and said . . . : Go take a lamb by your families, and sacrifice the Phase. And dip a bunch of hyssop in the blood . . . and sprinkle the transom of the door. . . . Let none of you go out of the door . . . till morning. For the Lord will pass through striking the Egyptians: and when He shall see the blood on the transom, and on both the posts, He will pass over the door of the house, and not suffer the destroyer ... to hurt you.

"Thou shalt keep this thing as a law for thee and thy children for ever."

Exodus 24:4-8

"And Moses wrote all the words of the Lord: and rising in the morning he built an altar at the foot of the mount. . . . And taking the book of the covenant, he read it in the hearing of the people: and they said: All things that the Lord hath spoken we will do, we will be obedient.

"And he took the blood and he sprinkled it upon the people, and he said: This is the blood of the covenant which the Lord hath made with you concerning all these words."

Exodus 29

The manner of consecrating Aaron and other priests.

c. Leviticus 1:4-13

"And he shall put his hand upon the head of the victim, and IT SHALL BE ACCEPTABLE and help to its expiation. And he shall immolate the calf before the Lord, and the priests, the sons of Aaron, shall offer the blood thereof, pouring it round about the altar, which is before the door of the tabernacle. . . .

"And the priest shall offer it all and burn it all upon the altar for a holocaust."
(See Hebrews 10:1-10)

Leviticus 23

The Lord speaks to Moses concerning the offering of sacrifices.

d. Numbers 12:8

"I speak to him [Moses] mouth to mouth; and plainly, and not by riddles and figures doth he see the Lord."

e. Psalm 109:4

"The Lord hath sworn, and He will not repent: THOU ART A PRIEST FOREVER ACCORDING TO THE ORDER OF MELCHISEDECH."

f. Luke 22:1-15

"Now the feast of unleavened bread, which is called THE PASCH was at hand ... on which it was necessary that the pasch should be killed. And He [Jesus] sent Peter and John saying: Go and prepare for us THE PASCH, that we may eat. . . . And when the hour was come, He sat down, and the twelve Apostles with Him."

2.   The Blood of the Cross

a. John 10:15, 18
"As the Father knoweth Me, and I know the Father: and I lay down my life for My sheep. No man taketh it away from Me: and I lay it down of Myself, and I have power to lay it down and I have power to take it up again. . . . "

b. Romans 5:9
"Christ died for us; much more therefore, being now justified by His blood, shall we be saved from wrath through Him."

c. Colossians 1:12-22
"Giving thanks to God the Father . . . Who hath delivered us from the power of darkness, and hath translated us into the kingdom of the Son of His love. In Whom we have redemption through His blood, the remission of sins: Who is the image of the invisible God, THE FIRST-BORN OF EVERY CREATURE. . . .

"And He is the head of the body, the Church, Who is the beginning, the first-born from the dead; that in all things He may hold the primacy. Because in Him it hath well pleased THE FATHER, that all fulness should dwell; and through Him to reconcile all things unto Himself, making peace through the blood of His cross. . . ."

Colossians 2:14
"Blotting out the handwriting of the decree that was against us, which was contrary to us. And he hath taken the same out of the way, fastening it to the cross."

d. I Timothy 2:5, 6
"FOR THERE IS ONE GOD, AND ONE MEDIATOR OF GOD AND MEN, THE MAN CHRIST JESUS: Who gave Himself a redemption for all, a testimony in due time."

e. I Peter 1:18, 19
"Knowing that you were not redeemed with corruptible things . . . but with the precious blood of Christ. . . . "

f. I John 1:7
"THE BLOOD OF JESUS CHRIST . . . CLEANSETH US FROM ALL SIN."

g. Apocalypse 1:5
"Jesus Christ . . . Who hath loved us and washed us from our sins in His own blood."

3. The Perpetual Sacrifice of the New Law

a. Malachias 1:10, 11

"... For from the rising of the sun even to the going down ... in every place there is sacrifice, and there is offered to My name a clean oblation. ...."

b. Matthew 26:26-28

"And on the first day of the Azymes, the disciples came to Jesus saying: Where wilt Thou that we prepare for Thee to eat the Pasch?

"... And whilst they were at supper Jesus took bread and blessed, and broke: and gave to His disciples and said: TAKE YE, AND EAT. THIS IS MY BODY. And taking the chalice, He gave thanks and gave to them, saying: DRINK YE ALL OF THIS. FOR THIS IS MY BLOOD OF THE NEW TESTAMENT, WHICH SHALL BE SHED FOR MANY UNTO THE REMISSION OF SINS" (Douay).

"And whilst they were eating, Jesus took bread, and blessed and broke and gave to the disciples saying, TAKE YE, EAT, THIS IS MY BODY.

"And He took a cup and after giving thanks He gave it to them, saying: DRINK YE ALL FROM IT; FOR THIS IS MY BLOOD, THE BLOOD OF THE COVENANT, WHICH IS BEING SHED FOR MANY UNTO THE FORGIVENESS OF SINS" (Westminster).

c. Mark 14:22-24

"And whilst they were eating Jesus took bread; and blessing broke and gave to them, and said: TAKE YE. THIS IS MY BODY. And having taken the chalice, giving thanks He gave it to them. And He said to them: THIS IS MY BLOOD OF THE NEW TESTAMENT, WHICH SHALL BE SHED FOR MANY" (Douay).

"And whilst they were eating He took bread and blessed ... and said: TAKE YE, THIS IS MY BODY.

"And He took a cup and giving thanks ... He said to them: THIS IS MY BLOOD OF THE COVENANT WHICH IS BEING SHED ON BEHALF OF MANY" (Westminster).

d. Luke 22:19, 20

"... And taking bread, He gave thanks and brake and gave to them saying: THIS IS MY BODY, WHICH IS GIVEN FOR YOU. DO THIS FOR A COMMEMORATION OF ME. In like

manner the chalice also ... saying: THIS IS THE CHALICE, THE
NEW TESTAMENT IN MY BLOOD WHICH SHALL BE SHED
FOR YOU" (Douay).

"And He took bread and gave thanks ... saying: THIS IS MY
BODY WHICH IS BEING GIVEN ON YOUR BEHALF; THIS
DO YE IN REMEMBRANCE OF ME.

"He took also the cup saying: THIS CUP IS THE NEW COVE-
NANT IN MY BLOOD, WHICH IS BEING SHED ON YOUR
BEHALF" (Westminster).

e. I Corinthians 11:23-29

" ... Jesus the same night in which He was betrayed took bread,

"And giving thanks broke, and said: TAKE YE AND EAT:
THIS IS MY BODY WHICH SHALL BE DELIVERED FOR YOU:
THIS DO FOR THE COMMEMORATION OF ME.

"In like manner also the chalice, after He had supped; saying:
THIS CHALICE IS THE NEW TESTAMENT IN MY BLOOD:
THIS DO YE, AS OFTEN AS YOU SHALL DRINK, FOR THE
COMMEMORATION OF ME. FOR AS OFTEN AS YOU SHALL
EAT THIS BREAD AND DRINK THE CHALICE, YOU SHALL
SHOW THE DEATH OF THE LORD, UNTIL HE COME. THERE-
FORE WHOSOEVER SHALL EAT THIS BREAD OR DRINK
THE CHALICE OF THE LORD UNWORTHILY SHALL BE
GUILTY OF THE BODY AND BLOOD OF THE LORD."

"But let a man prove himself; and so let him eat of that bread,
and drink of the chalice.

"For he that eateth and drinketh unworthily EATETH AND
DRINKETH JUDGMENT TO HIMSELF, NOT DISCERNING
THE BODY OF THE LORD" (Douay).

" ... the lord Jesus, on the night wherein He was being betrayed,
took bread, and giving thanks brake and said: THIS IS MY BODY,
WHICH (IS BEING GIVEN) ON YOUR BEHALF; THIS DO YE
IN REMEMBRANCE OF ME. In like manner after the supper
[He took] the cup saying: THIS CUP IS THE NEW COVENANT
IN MY BLOOD; THIS DO YE, AS OFTEN AS YOU DRINK
[THEREOF] IN REMEMBRANCE OF ME.

"For as often as you eat this bread and drink of the cup, you
proclaim the death of the Lord, until He come.

"So that whoever eateth the bread or drinketh of the cup of the
Lord unworthily, shall be guilty of the body and of the blood of the
Lord. But let a man prove himself, and so let him eat of the bread,
and drink of the cup; for he that eateth and drinketh without dis-
tinguishing the body [from other food] EATETH AND DRINKETH
JUDGMENT TO HIMSELF" (Westminster).

4. Jesus, Our Great Highpriest

a. Psalm 39:7-10

"Sacrifice and oblation Thou didst not desire. . . . Burnt offering and sin offering Thou didst not require; THEN SAID I, BEHOLD I COME.

"IN THE HEAD OF THE BOOK IT IS WRITTEN OF ME THAT I SHOULD DO THY WILL."

b. Romans 8:34

"Who is He that shall condemn? CHRIST JESUS, that died, yea, that is risen also again; WHO IS AT THE RIGHT HAND OF GOD, WHO ALSO MAKETH INTERCESSION FOR US."

c. Hebrews 2:17, 18

"Wherefore it behoved Him in all things to be made like unto His brethren, that He might become a merciful and faithful Highpriest before God, that He might be a propitiation for the sins of the people."

Hebrews 4:14-16

"Having therefore a great Highpriest that hath passed into the heavens, Jesus the Son of God: . . . For we have not a highpriest who cannot have compassion on our infirmities: but one tempted in all things like as we are, without sin. Let us go therefore with confidence to the throne of grace: that we may obtain mercy, and find grace in seasonable aid."

Hebrews 5:1-3

"For every highpriest taken from among men is ordained for men in the things that appertain to God, that he may offer up gifts and sacrifices for sins. . . ."

Hebrews 5:5

"So Christ also did not glorify Himself, that He might be made a highpriest; but He that said unto Him: Thou art My Son, this day have I begotten Thee."

Hebrews 7:1-3

"For this Melchisedech was king of Salem. . . . Without father, without mother, without genealogy, having neither beginning of days nor end of life, but likened unto the Son of God, continueth a priest forever."

Hebrews 7:22-27

" . . . Jesus . . . hath an everlasting priesthood, whereby He is able to save forever them that come to God by Him; always living to make intercession for us. For it was fitting that we should have such a Highpriest, holy, innocent, undefiled, separated from sinners, and made higher than the heavens. . . . "

Hebrews 8:3-8

"For every highpriest is appointed to offer gifts and sacrifices. . . . As it was answered to Moses. . . . See (saith He) that thou make all things according to the pattern which was shown thee on the Mount. But now He hath obtained a better ministry, by how much also He is a Mediator of a better testament, which is established on better promises."

Hebrews 9:11, 12

"But Christ, being come an Highpriest of the good things to come, by a greater and more perfect tabernacle not made with hand, that is, not of this creation.

"Neither by the blood of goats, or of calves, but by His own blood; entered once into the holies, having obtained eternal redemption."

Hebrews 9:24

"For Jesus is not entered into the holies made with hands . . . : but into heaven itself, THAT HE MAY APPEAR NOW IN THE PRESENCE OF GOD FOR US."

Hebrews 10:5-10

"Sacrifice and oblation Thou wouldst not: but a body Thou hast fitted to Me.

"Holocausts for sin did not please Thee. Then said I: Behold I come. In the head of the book it is written of Me: that I should do Thy will, O God. . . .

"Sacrifices, and oblations, and holocausts for sin Thou wouldst not, neither are they pleasing to Thee, which are offered according to the law. Then said I: Behold, I come to do Thy will, O God: He taketh away the first [the sacrifice of the Old Covenant] that He may establish that which followeth [the Sacrifice of the New Covenant]."

BOOKS FIVE AND SIX

The Sacraments

BASAL MATERIAL

FOR

DISCUSSING OR TEACHING

BOOKS FIVE AND SIX:
THE SACRAMENTS

177

Books Five and Six:

The Sacraments

A. INTRODUCTORY

Teaching Concerning Sin

Twenty years ago, conditions all over the world were very distressing.

The world was at war (1914-1918). And the horrors of this international catastrophe were the results of the inadequate teaching of Christ's principles throughout the world; that is, Christ's principles had not been taught in such a way as to bring about their assimilation and produce love in the souls of those who, in the main, were responsible for these horrors.

And it is a very sad fact that the vast number of people who did know and love Christ's principles were not strong enough in their INFLUENCE to bring about a just peace, and thus to prevent the awful suffering, desecration and bloodshed which the war entailed.

But I make bold to say that if Catholic teachers all over the world had consistently, over a long period of time, laid a careful, thorough foundation for First Holy Communion, together with such training of minds and wills that those minds and wills would REACT positively and steadily for the right; and if this type of teaching had been continued with these same children throughout the entire period of their Religious formation until they were mature and strong in Christ's principles; — their influence would undoubtedly have been so strong that, at least, the unnecessary cruelties of the World War might not have taken place, and certainly the unnecessary atrocities of modern warfare would not exist.

Throughout these last twenty years, Catholics have been growing more conscious that those distressing events took place because Christ's principles had not been taught in such a way as to cause minds and wills to react positively and constantly from the motive of love of God and neighbor instead of the motive of greed and love of power.

In the light of this knowledge there has been, of late, considerable agitation concerning the teaching of Christian Doctrine, and especially the preparation for First Holy Communion.

179

But it is amazing to look on and see how, in many, many places, the issue of right mind- and will-training, through a careful development of doctrine, is not taken into consideration. Too often there is hurried work in preparation merely for a special date or examination instead of preparation for growth in holiness. But is this not unfair to our Catholic people?

In spite of ourselves, we all feel forebodings as we look to the future. And I think the surest way to give the future a brighter outlook is to lay, in the souls of all of our children, a thorough, logical, systematic preparation for First Holy Communion; a preparation in which the minds and wills are trained to react vigorously for truth, justice and purity.

The mother or teacher who prepares the child for First Holy Communion has in her hands the very important task of giving the child its first ideas concerning the meaning of sin; thus she has in her hands the possibility of forming a conscience both delicate and true. The teaching given to the little child concerning sin should not be just the law and the keeping of the law. Rather, this fundamental teaching should be given to the child in the light of a personal relationship with God his Father, and with the idea of making the bond of love which exists between them sweeter and stronger.

Books Five and Six of the series, "A Little Child's First Communion," aim to give the child this type of teaching concerning sin, and such an understanding of Sanctifying Grace that he will be keen to grow in holiness through the loving reception of the Sacraments.

After this slow, solid development of the fundamental principles of our Faith has been given in preparation for First Holy Communion, then THE STATEMENTS IN THE CATECHISM should be just as carefully, logically and systematically developed; always aiming that the spiritual principle be so well assimilated that it will become a vital force permeating the child's decisions throughout his life.

This plan of teaching is the plan presented by Pope Pius X, as quoted on page 9.

B.   DOCTRINAL TRUTHS PRESENTED TO THE CHILD IN BOOKS FIVE AND SIX TEACH WITH THE EXPECTATION THAT HE WILL UNDERSTAND AND APPRECIATE THEM IN ACCORDANCE WITH HIS MENTAL AGE:

That:

1. Jesus must have loved us very, very much;

2. Jesus' Church gives us everything that we need to bring us into Heaven;

3. the possession of Sanctifying Grace is a more worth-while objective than any accomplishment;

4. when we lovingly receive the Sacraments of Jesus' Church, we are made holy by the gift of Sanctifying Grace; while if we already share in God's Love and Truth, Sanctifying Grace is increased in us.

C.   GROWTH IN POWER TO BE EXPECTED IN THE CHILD AS A RESULT OF STUDYING BOOKS FIVE AND SIX:

Greater facility:

1. in interpreting the printed page;

2. in grasping more difficult subject-matter;

3. in frequenting the Sacraments of Penance and Holy Eucharist;

4. in realizing the evil of sin;

5. in making more fervent Acts of Contrition;

6. in speaking easily and naturally on subjects pertaining to Jesus and His Church;

7. in reading religious books;

8. in interior conversation with God.

D. PEDAGOGICAL STRUCTURE

The point called application belongs to the pedagogical structure of the lesson, and the assimilation of the doctrinal principle being taught will be more thorough if the teacher concludes the teaching of the unit with applications involving this doctrinal principle.

These applications may be varied to include devotional practices flowing from an understanding of the doctrine taught; music, art or sculpture related to this doctrine; and the individual illustrated doctrinal notebook.

In the study of the Sacraments, the applications should be varied and thorough. Special attention is given to this pedagogical point in Books Five and Six of "A Little Child's First Communion," and this will be noticed in the study of the following outline.

Teacher's Major Objective

To create in the child a desire for greater holiness through a deeper appreciation of Sanctifying Grace and the Sacraments.

Exploration and Establishment of an Apperceptive

Background for the New Knowledge

This part of the lesson is an exploration into the child's mind to discover what he already knows which would dovetail into the new subject-matter about to be presented and establish an appropriate apperceptive background for it.

a. Jesus is All-Holy.

b. To be more like Jesus, you must have more of God's Love and Truth in you.

c. Jesus gives us of God's Love and Truth through the Sacraments of the Church He left us.

Motivation

The introductory page, Book Five, gives a child's motivation for studying Book Five.

The introductory page, Book Six, gives a child's motivation for studying Book Six.

Presentation of New Knowledge

Generalizations

a. God's Own Son gives us of God's Love and Truth (Sanctifying Grace) through the Sacraments of the Church He left us.

b. Any act against God is called a sin. All sins mean that the one who commits the sin is not giving to "the Living God" all the love which should be given to Him.

c. The seven Sacraments of Jesus' Church are: Baptism, Confirmation, Penance, Holy Eucharist, Extreme Unction, Holy Orders and Matrimony.
Baptism is the Sacrament which gives us God's sanctifying Grace for the first time, and makes us God's children.
Confirmation is the Sacrament which gives us more of the power of the Holy Ghost, and makes us soldiers of Jesus' Church.
Penance is the Sacrament which we receive when Jesus' priest forgives our sins if we are truly sorry for them.
Holy Eucharist is the Sacrament which we receive at Holy Communion when Jesus comes to live within us.
Extreme Unction is the Sacrament which we receive when we are very sick to prepare us for Heaven.
Holy Orders is the Sacrament which men receive at the time they are becoming Jesus' priests.
Matrimony is the Sacrament which a man and woman receive at the time of their marriage.

d. Heaven is Jesus' Kingdom. Those who receive Holy Communion lovingly all their lives will be in Jesus' Kingdom forever.

Applications and Related Activities

E. THEOLOGICAL BACKGROUND

When any teacher of doctrine who has not previously verified the knowledge in his own mind begins to study the "Summa" of St. Thomas concerning any dogma, he is likely, after his study, to feel that it is only then that he has begun to understand the doctrine.

But when this consciousness has been attained, there will be a stability and strength to his teaching which were not there before.

The following texts concerning the Sacraments are, in the main, from the writings of St. Thomas.

1. The Sacraments

a. "A sacrament properly speaking is that which is ordained to signify our sanctification. In which three things may be considered; viz., the very cause of our sanctification, which is Christ's Passion; the form of our sanctification, which is grace and the virtues; and the ultimate end of our sanctification, which is eternal life. And all these are signified by the sacraments. Consequently a sacrament is a sign that is both A REMINDER OF THE PAST, i. e., THE PASSION OF CHRIST; and AN INDICATION OF THAT WHICH IS EFFECTED IN US BY CHRIST'S PASSION, i. e., GRACE; and A PROGNOSTIC, THAT IS A FORETELLING OF FUTURE GLORY."

St. Thomas Aquinas,
"Summa Theologica," Part Three, Third Number, Q. LX, Art. III.

b. "Now it is part of man's nature to acquire knowledge of the intelligible from the sensible. But a sign is that by means of which one attains to the knowledge of something else. Consequently, since THE SACRED THINGS WHICH ARE SIGNIFIED BY THE SACRAMENTS ARE THE SPIRITUAL AND INTELLIGIBLE GOODS BY MEANS OF WHICH MAN IS SANCTIFIED, it follows that the sacramental signs consist in sensible things: just as, in the Divine Scriptures, spiritual things are set before us under the guise of things sensible. And hence it is that sensible things are required for the sacraments; as Dionysius also proves in his book on the heavenly hierarchy ('Coel. Hier.,' I)."

Ibid., Art. IV.

c. "Sacraments are necessary for man's salvation, in so far as they are SENSIBLE SIGNS OF INVISIBLE THINGS whereby man is made holy."

Ibid., Q. LXI, Art. III.

d. "In the use of the sacraments two things may be considered, namely, the worship of God, and the sanctification of man: the former of which pertains to man as referred to God, and the latter pertains to God in reference to man. Now it is not for anyone to determine that which is in the power of another, but only that which is in his own power. Since, therefore, the sanctification of man is in the power of God Who sanctifies, IT IS NOT FOR MAN TO DECIDE WHAT THINGS SHOULD BE USED FOR HIS SANCTI-FICATION, BUT THIS SHOULD BE DETERMINED BY DIVINE INSTITUTION. Therefore in the sacraments of the New Law, by which man is sanctified, according to 1 Corinthians 6:11, 'You are washed, you are sanctified,' we must use those things which are determined by Divine institution."

Ibid., Q. LX, Art. V.

e. "Sacraments may be considered on the part of man who is sanctified, and who is composed of soul and body: to whom the sacramental remedy is adjusted, since it touches the body through the sensible element, and the soul through faith in the words. Hence Augustine says ('Tract. LXXX in Joan.'), 'Now you are clean by reason of the word,' etc. Whence hath water this so great virtue, to touch the body and wash the heart, but by the word doing it, not because it is spoken, but because it is believed?"

Ibid., Art. VI.

f. "Water may signify both a cleansing by reason of its humidity, and refreshment by reason of its being cool: but when we say, 'I baptize thee,' it is clear that we use water in Baptism in order to signify a spiritual cleansing."

Ibid.

g. "Sacraments are necessary unto man's salvation for three reasons. The first is taken from the condition of human nature, which is such that it has to be led by things corporeal and sensible to things spiritual and intelligible. Now it belongs to Divine Providence to provide for each one according as its condition requires. DIVINE WISDOM, THEREFORE, FITTINGLY PROVIDES MAN WITH MEANS OF SALVATION, IN THE SHAPE OF CORPOREAL AND SENSIBLE SIGNS THAT ARE CALLED SACRAMENTS.

"The second reason is taken from the state of man who in sinning subjected himself by his affections to corporeal things. Now the healing remedy should be given to a man so as to reach the part affected by disease. Consequently it was fitting that God should provide man with a spiritual medicine by means of certain corporeal signs; for if man were offered spiritual things without a veil, his mind being taken up with the material world would be unable to apply itself to them.

"The third reason is taken from the fact that man is prone to direct his activity chiefly toward material things. Lest, therefore, it should be too hard for man to be drawn away entirely from bodily actions, bodily exercise was offered to him in the sacraments, by which he might be trained to avoid superstitious practices, consisting in the worship of demons, and all manner of harmful action, consisting in sinful deeds.

"It follows, therefore, that through the institution of the sacraments man, consistently with his nature, is instructed through sensible things; he is humbled, through confessing that he is subject to corporeal things, seeing that he receives assistance through them: and he is even preserved from bodily hurt, by the healthy exercise of the sacraments."

Ibid., Q. LXI, Art. I.

h. "Christ's Passion is a sufficient cause of man's salvation. But it does not follow that the sacraments are not also necessary for that purpose: because THEY OBTAIN THEIR EFFECT THROUGH THE POWER OF CHRIST'S PASSION; and Christ's Passion is, so to say, applied to man through the sacraments according to the Apostle (Romans 6:3): 'All we who are baptized in Christ Jesus, are baptized in His death.'"

Ibid.

i. "Augustine says ('Contra Faust.,' XIX) the sacraments of things present should be different from sacraments of things to come. Now the sacraments of the Old Law foretold the coming of Christ. Consequently they did not signify Christ so clearly as the sacraments of the New Law, which flow from Christ Himself, and have a certain likeness to Him."

Ibid., Q. LX, Art. VI.

j. "As the ancient Fathers were saved through faith in Christ's future coming, so we are saved through faith in Christ's past birth and Passion. Now the sacraments are signs in protestation of the faith whereby man is justified."

Ibid., Q. LXI, Art. IV.

k. "The prayers which are said in giving the sacraments, are offered to God, not on the part of the individual, but on the part of the whole Church, whose prayers are acceptable to God, according to Matthew 18:19."

Ibid., Q. LXIV, Art. I.

l. "But that which is the sacramental effect is not impetrated by the prayer of the Church or of the minister, BUT THROUGH THE MERIT OF CHRIST'S PASSION, THE POWER OF WHICH OPERATES IN THE SACRAMENTS."

Ibid.

m. "We must needs say that in some way the sacraments of the New Law cause grace. For it is evident that through the sacraments of the New Law man is incorporated with Christ: thus the Apostle says of Baptism (Galatians 3:27) : 'As many of you as have been baptized in Christ have put on Christ.' And MAN IS MADE A MEMBER OF CHRIST THROUGH GRACE ALONE."

Ibid., Q. LXII, Art. I.

n. "We have it on authority of many saints that the sacraments of the New Law not only signify, BUT ALSO CAUSE GRACE."

Ibid.

o. "As stated in the Second Part (I-II, Q. CX, AA. 3, 4), grace, considered in itself, perfects the essence of the soul, in so far as it is a certain participated likeness of the Divine Nature. And just as the soul's powers flow from its essence, so from grace there flow certain perfections into the powers of the soul, which are called virtues and gifts, whereby the powers are perfected in reference to their actions. Now the sacraments are ordained unto certain special effects which are necessary in the Christian life: thus Baptism is ordained unto a certain spiritual regeneration, by which man dies to vice and becomes a member of Christ: which effect is something special in addition to the actions of the souls' powers: and the same holds true of the other sacraments. Consequently just as the virtues and gifts confer, in addition to grace commonly so called, a certain special perfection ordained to the powers' proper actions, so does sacramental grace confer, over and above grace commonly so called, and in addition to the virtues and gifts, a certain Divine assistance in obtaining the end of the sacrament. It is thus that sacramental grace confers something in addition to the grace of the virtues and gifts."

Ibid., Q. LXII, Art. II.

p. "The sacraments of the New Law are ordained for a twofold purpose, namely, as a remedy for sin, and for the Divine worship. All the sacraments, from the fact that they confer grace, have this in common, that they afford a remedy against sin: whereas not all the sacraments are directly ordained to the Divine worship. Thus it is clear that penance, whereby man is delivered from sin, does not afford man any advance in the Divine worship, but restores him to his former state."

Ibid., Q. LXIII, Art. VI.

q. "We may likewise gather the number of the sacraments from their being instituted as a remedy against the defect caused by sin. For Baptism is intended as a remedy against the absence of spiritual life; Confirmation, against the infirmity of soul found in those of recent birth; the Eucharist against the soul's proneness to sin; Penance against actual sin committed after Baptism; Extreme Unction against the remainders of sins — of those sins namely, which are not sufficiently removed by Penance, whether through negligence or through ignorance; Order, against divisions in the community; Matrimony, as a remedy against concupiscence in the individual, and against the decrease in numbers that results from death."

Ibid., Q. LXV, Art. I.

r. "Some, again, gather the number of sacraments from a certain adaptation to the virtues and to the defects and penal effects resulting from sin. They say that Baptism corresponds to Faith, and is ordained as a remedy against original sin; Extreme Unction to Hope, being ordained against venial sin; the Eucharist to Charity, being ordained against the penal effect which is malice; Order to Prudence, being ordained against ignorance; Penance to Justice, being ordained against mortal sin; Matrimony to Temperance, being ordained against concupiscence; Confirmation to Fortitude, being ordained against infirmity."

Ibid.

2. Baptism

a. "Circumcision was a preparation for Baptism, inasmuch as it was a profession of faith in Christ, which we also profess in Baptism."

Ibid., Q. LXX, Art. II.

b. "Grace was bestowed in circumcision as to all the effects of grace, but not as in Baptism. Because in Baptism grace is bestowed by the very power of Baptism itself, which power Baptism has as the instrument of Christ's Passion already consummated."

Ibid., Art. IV.

c. "Our Lord enjoined on the Apostles, whose place is taken by the bishops, both duties, namely, of teaching and baptizing, but in different ways."

Ibid., Q. LXVII, Art. II.

d. "BAPTISM IS THE SACRAMENT OF FAITH: since it is a profession of the Christian faith. Now in order that a man receive the Faith, he must be instructed therein, according to Romans 10:14. And therefore it is fitting that catechism should precede Baptism. Hence when our Lord bade His disciples to baptize, He made teaching to precede Baptism, saying: GO YE, ... AND TEACH ALL NATIONS, BAPTIZing THEM," etc.

Ibid., Q. LXXI, Art. I.

e. "In the Sacrament of Baptism, three things may be considered: namely, that which is sacrament only; that which is reality and sacrament; and that which is reality only. That which is sacrament only, is something visible and outward; the sign, namely, of the inward effect: for such is the very nature of a sacrament."

Ibid., Q. LXVI, Art. I.

f. "The intention is essential to Baptism."
> Ibid., Art. VIII.

g. "An unbaptized person cannot be a godparent, as was decreed in the Council of Mainz, although an unbaptized person may baptize."
> Ibid., Q. LXVII, Art. VIII.

h. "Man receives the forgiveness of sins before Baptism in so far as he has Baptism of desire, explicitly or implicitly; and yet when he actually receives Baptism, he receives a fuller remission, as to the remission of the entire punishment."
> Ibid., Q. LXIX, Art. IV.

i. "It is clear that the Passion of Christ is communicated to every baptized person, so that he is healed just as if he himself had suffered and died. Now Christ's Passion, as stated above (Q. LXVIII, Art. V), is a sufficient satisfaction for all the sins of all men. CONSEQUENTLY HE WHO IS BAPTIZED, IS FREED FROM THE DEBT OF ALL PUNISHMENT DUE TO HIM FOR HIS SINS, JUST AS IF HE HIMSELF HAD OFFERED SUFFICIENT SATISFACTION FOR ALL HIS SINS."
> Ibid., Art. II.

j. "Baptism is a remedy not only against original sin, but also against actual sins, which are caused by our will and intention."
> Ibid., Q. LXVIII, Art. VII.

k. "The least baptismal grace suffices to blot out all sins."
> Ibid., Q. LXIX, Art. VIII.

l. "To open the gates of the heavenly kingdom is to remove the obstacle that prevents one from entering therein. Now this obstacle is guilt and the debt of punishment. But it has been shown above (AA. I, 2) that all guilt and also all debt of punishment are taken away by Baptism. It follows, therefore, that the effect of Baptism is to open the gates of the heavenly kingdom. Baptism opens the gates of the heavenly kingdom to the baptized in so far as it incorporates them in the Passion of Christ, by applying its power to man."
> Ibid., Art. VII.

m. "The effect of Baptism is to take away, not future, but present and past sins. And consequently, when the insincerity passes away, subsequent sins are indeed remitted, but by Penance, not by Baptism. Wherefore they are not remitted, like the sins which preceded Baptism, as to the whole debt of punishment."
> Ibid., Art. X.

n. "Baptism is conferred principally as a remedy against original sin. Wherefore, just as original sin is not renewed, SO NEITHER IS BAPTISM REITERATED...."

Ibid., Q. LXVI, Art. IX.

o. "As Augustine says, even apostates are not deprived of their Baptism, for when they repent and return to the fold they do not receive it again; whence we conclude that it cannot be lost."

Ibid., Q. LXIII, Art. V.

p. "Although external worship does not last after this life, yet its end remains. Consequently, after this life the character remains, both in the good as adding to their glory, and in the wicked as increasing their shame."

Ibid.

q. "A character exists in the soul in an indelible manner, not from any perfection of its own, but from the perfection of Christ's Priesthood, from which the character flows like an instrumental power."

Ibid.

r. "Augustine ('Ad Fortunatum'), speaking of the comparison between Baptisms, says: 'The newly baptized confesses his faith in the presence of a priest: the martyr in the presence of the persecutor. The former is sprinkled with water, after he has confessed; the latter with his blood. The former receives the Holy Ghost by the imposition of the bishop's hands; the latter is made the temple of the Holy Ghost.'"

Ibid., Q. LXVI, Art. XII.

s. "'THE TEMPLE OF GOD IS HOLY, WHICH YOU ARE' (1 Corinthians 3:17); THAT IS, ALL WHO BELIEVE IN CHRIST, AND SO BELIEVE AS TO LOVE; not as the devils believed (James 2:19), who loved not; and therefore, though they believed, cried, 'What have we to do with Thee, Jesus Son of God?' (Matthew 8:29). But we, let us so believe that we may believe in Him, loving Him, and may not say, 'What have we to do with Thee?' but may rather say, 'Unto Thee we belong; Thou hast redeemed us.'"

St. Augustine, "In Ps. CXXX," 1.

t. "Do thou all within. And if perchance thou seekest some high place, some holy place, make thee a temple for God within. For 'the temple of God is holy: which you are' (1 Corinthians 3:17). In a temple wouldst thou pray? Pray within thyself. ONLY FIRST BE THOU A TEMPLE OF GOD, because He in His temple will hear him that prayeth."

St. Augustine, "In Joan. Evang.," XV, 25.

3. Confirmation

a. "So therefore does man receive spiritual life in Baptism, which is a spiritual regeneration: while in Confirmation man arrives at the perfect age, as it were, of the spiritual life. Hence Pope Melchiades says: 'THE HOLY GHOST, WHO COMES DOWN ON THE WATERS OF BAPTISM BEARING SALVATION IN HIS FLIGHT, BE-STOWS AT THE FOUNT THE FULNESS OF INNOCENCE; BUT IN CONFIRMATION HE CONFERS AN INCREASE OF GRACE. IN BAPTISM WE ARE BORN AGAIN UNTO LIFE; AFTER BAP-TISM WE ARE STRENGTHENED.' And therefore it is evident that Confirmation is a special sacrament.

St. Thomas Aquinas, loc. cit., Q. LXXII, Art. I.

b. "Confirmation is the sacrament of the fulness of grace: wherefore there could be nothing corresponding to it in the Old Law, since the Law brought nothing to perfection (Hebrews 7:19)."

Ibid., Q. LXXII, Art. I.

c. "And this Sacrament of Confirmation is, as it were, the final completion of the Sacrament of Baptism; in the sense that by Baptism man is built up into a spiritual dwelling, and is written like a spiritual letter; whereas by the Sacrament of Confirmation, like a house already built, he is consecrated as a temple of the Holy Ghost, and as a letter already written, is signed with the sign of the cross. Therefore the conferring of this sacrament is reserved to bishops, who possess supreme power in the Church: just as in the primitive Church, the fulness of the Holy Ghost was given by the Apostles, in whose place the bishops stand (Acts 8). Hence Pope Urban I says: 'ALL THE FAITHFUL SHOULD, AFTER BAPTISM, RECEIVE THE HOLY GHOST BY THE IMPOSITION OF THE BISHOP'S HAND, THAT THEY MAY BECOME PERFECT CHRISTIANS."

Ibid., Art. XI.

d. "Baptism is the regeneration unto the spiritual life, whereby man lives in himself. And therefore in the baptismal form that action alone is expressed which refers to the man to be sanctified. But this sacrament is ordained not only to the sanctification of man in himself, but also to strengthen him in his outward combat. Consequently not only is men-tion made of interior sanctification, in the words, 'I confirm thee with the chrism of salvation'; but furthermore man is signed outwardly, as it were with the standard of the cross, unto the outward spiritual com-bat; and this signified by the words, 'I sign thee with the sign of the cross.'"

Ibid., Art. IV.

e. "IN THIS SACRAMENT THE HOLY GHOST IS GIVEN TO THE BAPTIZED FOR STRENGTH: just as He was given to the Apostles on the day of Pentecost, as we read in Acts 2; and just as He was given to the baptized by the imposition of the Apostles' hands, as related in Acts 8:17. Now it has been proved in the First Part that the Holy Ghost is not sent or given except with sanctifying grace. Consequently it is evident that sanctifying grace is bestowed in this sacrament."

Ibid., Art. VII.

f. "The character of Confirmation of necessity supposes the baptismal character: so that, in effect, if one who is not baptized were to be confirmed, he would receive nothing, but would have to be confirmed again after receiving Baptism. The reason of this is that, Confirmation is to Baptism as growth to birth."

Ibid., Art. VI.

g. "Chrism is the fitting matter of this sacrament. For, as stated above (A. I), IN THIS SACRAMENT THE FULNESS OF THE HOLY GHOST IS GIVEN for the spiritual strength which belongs to the perfect age. Now, when man comes to perfect age he begins at once to have intercourse with others; whereas until then he lives an individual life, as it were, confined to himself. Now the grace of the Holy Ghost is signified by oil; hence Christ is said to be anointed with the oil of gladness (Psalm 44:8), by reason of His being gifted with the fulness of the Holy Ghost. Consequently oil is a suitable matter of this sacrament. And balm is mixed with the oil, by reason of its fragrant odor, which spreads about: hence the Apostle says (2 Corinthians 2:15): 'We are the good odor of Christ,' etc. And though many other things be fragrant, yet preference is given to balm, because it has a special odor of its own, and because it confers incorruptibility: hence it is written (Ecclesiasticus 24:21): 'My odor is as the purest balm.' "

Ibid., Q. LXII, Art. II.

4. Sin

a. "THE WILL THAT TURNS AWAY FROM THE IMMUTABLE GOOD COMMON TO ALL AND TURNS TOWARD ITS OWN GOOD, WHETHER OUTWARD TO ITSELF OR DOWNWARD, SINS. It turns toward its own when it wills to be its own master; toward outward good, when out of curiosity it strives to know things which are the property of others, or which do not pertain to itself; to the lower good, when it loves the pleasures of the body. And in this way man, having become proud and inquisitive and licentious, is taken captive by another life, which in comparison with the higher life is death."

St. Augustine, "De lib. arb.," 11, xix, 35.

b. "As stated in Ecclesiasticus 10:15, PRIDE IS THE BEGINNING OF ALL SIN, because thereby man clings to his own judgment, and strays from the Divine Commandments."

St. Thomas Aquinas, op. cit.,
Supp. Part Three, Book Four, Q. I., Art. I.

c. "Whatever we are forbidden by God's law, and whatever we are bidden to do, comes under two commandments: . . . the general prohibition, 'Thou shalt not covet' (Exodus 20:7), and the general precept, 'Thou shalt love' (Deuteronomy 6:5). . . . By eschewing covetousness we put off the old man, and by showing love we put on the new."

St. Augustine, "De perf. just. hominis," v, 11.

d. "As stated above (Q. LXXXVI, A. 4), mortal sin contains two things, aversion from God and adherence to a created good. Now, in mortal sin, whatever attaches to the aversion is, considered in itself, common to all mortal sins, SINCE MAN TURNS AWAY FROM GOD BY EVERY MORTAL SIN, so that, in consequence, the stain resulting from the privation of grace, and the debt of everlasting punishment, are common to all mortal sins. This is what is meant by what is written (James 2:10): 'WHOSOEVER . . . SHALL OFFEND IN ONE POINT, IS BECOME GUILTY OF ALL.' "

St. Thomas Aquinas, op. cit.,
Part Three, Fourth Number, Q. LXXXVIII, Art. I.

e. "Every actual sin is caused by our will not yielding to God's law, either by transgressing it, or by omitting it, or by acting beside it: and since a hard thing is one that is disposed not to give way easily, hence it is that a certain hardness of the will is to be found in every actual sin. WHEREFORE, IF A SIN IS TO BE REMEDIED, IT NEEDS TO BE TAKEN AWAY BY CONTRITION WHICH CRUSHES IT."

Ibid., Supp. Part Three, Book Four, Q. II, Art. III.

f. "Mortal sin, in so far as it turns inordinately to a mutable good, produces in the soul a certain disposition, or even a habit, if the acts be repeated frequently. Now it has been said above . . . that the guilt of mortal sin is pardoned through grace removing the aversion of the mind from God. Nevertheless, when that which is on the part of the aversion has been taken away by grace, that which is on the part of the inordinate turning to a mutable good can remain."

Ibid., Part Three, Fourth Number, Q. LXXXVI, Art. V.

g. "As stated above (Q. I., A. II, ad I), there is a twofold sorrow in contrition: one is in the will, and is the very essence of contrition."

Ibid., Supp. Part Three, Book Four, Q. III, Art. I.

h. "As stated in the Second Part (I, II., Q. LXXXVII, A. 4), IN
    MORTAL SIN THERE ARE TWO THINGS, NAMELY, A TURN-
    ING FROM THE IMMUTABLE GOOD, AND AN INORDINATE
    TURNING TO MUTABLE GOOD. Accordingly, in so far as mortal
    sin turns away from immutable Good, it induces a debt of eternal
    punishment, so that whosoever sins against the eternal Good should
    be punished eternally. Again, in so far as mortal sin turns inordinately
    to a mutable good, it gives rise to a debt of some punishment, because
    the disorder of guilt is not brought back to the order of justice, except
    by punishment: since it is just that he who has been too indulgent to
    his will should suffer something against his will, for thus will equality
    be restored. Hence it is written (Apocalypse 18:7): 'As much as she
    hath glorified herself, and lived in delicacies, so much torment and
    sorrow give ye to her.'

       "Since, however, the turning to mutable good is finite, sin does not,
    in this respect, induce a debt of eternal punishment. Wherefore, if man
    turns inordinately to a mutable good without turning from God, as
    happens in venial sins, he incurs a debt, not of eternal but of temporal
    punishment. CONSEQUENTLY, WHEN GUILT IS PARDONED
    THROUGH GRACE, THE SOUL CEASES TO BE TURNED AWAY
    FROM GOD, THROUGH BEING UNITED TO GOD BY GRACE;
    so that at the same time, the debt of punishment is taken away, albeit
    a debt of some temporal punishment may yet remain."

                                          Ibid., Q. LXXXVI, Art. IV.

i   "No infusion of fresh grace is required for the forgiveness of a venial
    sin, but it is enough to have an act proceeding from grace, in detesta-
    tion of that venial sin, either explicit or at least implicit, as when one
    is moved fervently to God. Hence, for three reasons, certain things
    cause the remission of venial sins: First, because they imply the infusion
    of grace, since the infusion of grace removes venial sins, as stated above
    . . . ; and so, by the Eucharist, Extreme Unction, and by all the
    sacraments of the New Law without exception, wherein grace is con-
    ferred, venial sins are remitted. Secondly, because they imply a move-
    ment of detestation for sin, and in this way the general confession
    [i. e., the recital of the Confiteor or of an Act of Contrition], the
    beating of one's breast, and the Lord's Prayer conduce to the remis-
    sion of venial sins, for we ask in the Lord's Prayer: 'Forgive us our tres-
    passes.' Thirdly, because they include a movement of reverence for
    God and divine things; and in this way a bishop's blessing, the sprin-
    kling of holy water, any sacramental anointing, a prayer said in a dedi-
    cated church, and anything else of the kind, conduce to the remission
    of venial sins."

                                          Ibid., Q. LXXXVII, Art. III.

5. The Sacrament of Penance

a. "Christ's Passion, without whose power neither original sin nor actual sin is remitted, produces its effect in us through the reception of the sacraments which derive their efficacy from it. Wherefore, for the remission of both actual and original sin a sacrament of the Church is necessary, received either actually, or at least in desire, when a man fails to receive the sacrament actually through an unavoidable obstacle, and not through contempt. Consequently those sacraments which are ordained as remedies for sin, which is incompatible with salvation, are necessary for salvation: and so, just as Baptism, whereby original sin is blotted out, is necessary for salvation, so also is the Sacrament of Penance."

Ibid., Q. VI, Art. I.

b. "AS GREGORY SAYS (*loc. cit.*), A SACRAMENT CONSISTS IN A SOLEMN ACT WHEREBY SOMETHING IS SO DONE THAT WE UNDERSTAND IT TO SIGNIFY THE HOLINESS WHICH IT CONFERS. Now it is evident that in Penance something is done so that something holy is signified both on the part of the penitent sinner and on the part of the priest absolving; because the penitent sinner, by deed and word, shows his heart to have renounced sin, and in like manner the priest, by his deed and word with regard to the penitent, signifies the work of God Who forgives his sins. Therefore it is evident that Penance, as practised in the Church, is a sacrament."

Ibid., Part Three, Fourth Number, Q. LXXXIV, Art. I.

c. "GOD ALONE ABSOLVES FROM SIN AND FORGIVES SINS AUTHORITATIVELY; yet priests do both ministerially, because the words of the priest in this sacrament work as instruments of the Divine power, as in the other sacraments: because it is the Divine power that works inwardly in all the sacramental signs, be they things or words."

Ibid., Art. III.

d. "Penance is ordained to man's salvation accidentally as it were, and on something being supposed, viz., sin: for unless man were to sin actually, he would not stand in need of Penance, and yet he would need Baptism, Confirmation and the Eucharist."

Ibid., Art. VI.

e. "Penance regards every kind of sin in a way, but not each in the same way. Because Penance regards actual mortal sin properly and chiefly; properly, since, properly speaking, we are said to repent of what we have done of our own will; chiefly, since this sacrament was instituted chiefly for the blotting out of mortal sin. PENANCE REGARDS VENIAL SINS, PROPERLY SPEAKING INDEED, IN SO FAR AS THEY ARE COMMITTED OF OUR OWN WILL, BUT THIS WAS NOT THE CHIEF PURPOSE OF ITS INSTITUTION."

Ibid., Art. II.

f. "Forgiveness of sin, as stated above (Q. LXXXVI, A. 2), is effected by man being united to God from Whom sin separates him in some way. Now this separation is made complete by mortal sin, and incomplete by venial sin: because, by mortal sin, THE MIND THROUGH ACTING AGAINST CHARITY IS ALTOGETHER TURNED AWAY FROM GOD; whereas by venial sin man's affections are clogged, so that they are slow in tending toward God. Consequently both kinds of sin are taken away by penance, because BY BOTH OF THEM MAN'S WILL IS DISORDERED THROUGH TURNING INORDINATELY TO A CREATED GOOD; for just as mortal sin cannot be forgiven so long as the will is attached to sin, so neither can venial sin, because while the cause remains, the effect remains."

Ibid., Q. LXXXVII, Art. I.

g. "Sins are pardoned through Penance, as stated above (Q. LXXXVI, A. I). But there can be no remission of sins except through the infusion of grace. Wherefore it follows that grace is infused into man through Penance. Now all the gratuitous virtues flow from grace, even as all the powers result from the essence of the soul, as stated in the Second Part (I, II, Q. CX, A. 4 ad I). Therefore all the virtues are restored through Penance."

Ibid., Q. LXXXIX, Art. I.

6. Confession

a. "We are bound to confession on two counts: first, by the Divine law, from the very fact that confession is a remedy, and in this way not all are bound to confession, but those only who fall into mortal sin after Baptism; secondly, by a precept of positive law, and in this way all are bound by the precept of the Church laid down in the general council (Later. IV, Can. 21) under Innocent III, both IN ORDER THAT EVERYONE MAY ACKNOWLEDGE HIMSELF TO BE A SINNER, BECAUSE ALL HAVE SINNED AND NEED THE GRACE OF GOD (Romans 3:23); and that the Eucharist may be approached with greater reverence."

Ibid., Supp. Third Part, Book Four, Q. VI, Art. III.

b. "By venial sin man is separated neither from God nor from the sacraments of the Church: wherefore he does not need to receive any further grace for the forgiveness of such a sin, nor does he need to be reconciled to the Church. Consequently a man does not need to confess his venial sins to a priest."

Ibid., Q. VIII, Art. III.

c. "Each thing is removed by its contrary. But venial sin is not contrary to habitual grace or charity, BUT HAMPERS ITS ACT, through man being too much attached to a created good, albeit not in opposition to God, as stated in the Second Part (I, II, Q. LXXXVIII, A. I; II, II, Q. XXIV, Art. 10). Therefore, in order that venial sin be removed, it is not necessary that habitual grace be infused, but a movement of grace or charity suffices for its forgiveness. Nevertheless, since in those who have the use of free-will (in whom alone can there be venial sin), there can be no infusion of grace without an actual movement of the free-will toward God and against sin, consequently whenever grace is infused anew, venial sins are forgiven. . . . Venial sin is never forgiven without some act, explicit or implicit, of the virtue of penance, as stated above (A. I); it can, however, be forgiven without the Sacrament of Penance, which is formally perfected by the priestly absolution."

Ibid., Part Three, Fourth Number, Q. LXXXVII, Art. II.

d. "Confession produces its effect, ON THE PRESUPPOSITION THAT THERE IS CONTRITION which blots out guilt."

Ibid., Supp. Part Three, Book Four, Q. X., Art. V.

e. "Penance is twofold, internal and external. Internal penance is that whereby one grieves for a sin one has committed, and this penance should last until the end of life."

Ibid., Part Three, Fourth Number, Q. LXXXIV, Art. VIII.

f. "External penance is that whereby a man shows external signs of sorrow, confesses his sins verbally to the priest who absolves him, and makes satisfaction for his sins according to the judgment of the priest."

Ibid.

g. "Now this sacrament, namely the Sacrament of Penance, consists not in the consecration of a matter, nor in the use of a hallowed matter, but rather in the removal of a certain matter, viz., sin, in so far as sins are said to be the matter of Penance, as explained above (Art. II). This removal is expressed by the priest: I ABSOLVE THEE."

Ibid., Art. III.

h. "The grace that is given in the sacraments descends from the Head to the members. Wherefore he alone who exercises a ministry over Christ's true body is a minister of the sacraments, wherein grace is given; and this belongs to a priest alone, who can consecrate the Eucharist. Therefore, since grace is given in the Sacrament of Penance, none but a priest is the minister of the sacrament: and consequently sacramental confession which should be made to a minister of the Church, should be made to none but a priest."

Ibid., Supp. Part Three, Book Four, Q. VIII, Art. I.

i. "... The power of forgiving sins was entrusted to priests; not that they may forgive them by their own power, FOR THIS BELONGS TO GOD, but that, as ministers, they may declare the operation of God Who forgives."

Ibid., Q. XVIII, Art. I.

j. "It is written (Matthew 16:19), TO THEE WILL I GIVE THE KEYS OF THE KINGDOM OF HEAVEN.

"Further, every dispenser should have the keys of the things that he dispenses. But the ministers of the Church are the dispensers of the divine mysteries, as appears from 1 Corinthians 4:1. Therefore they ought to have the keys.

"... I answer that in material things a key is an instrument for opening a door. Now the door of the kingdom is closed to us through sin, both as to the stain and as to the debt of punishment. Wherefore the power of removing this obstacle is called a key."

Ibid., Q. XVII, Art. I.

k. "The operation of the priest in using the keys is conformed to God's operation, Whose minister he is. NOW GOD'S OPERATION EXTENDS BOTH TO GUILT AND TO PUNISHMENT."

Ibid., Q. XVIII, Art. III.

l. "Satisfaction is a part of Penance as a sacrament, and a fruit of penance as a virtue."

Ibid., Part Three, Fourth Number, Q. XC, Art. II.

m. "As stated in the Second Part (I-II, Q. CIX, AA. 7, 8; Q. CXI, A. 2), it belongs to grace to co-operate with man that his work may be rightly done. Consequently the forgiveness of guilt and of the debt of eternal punishment belongs to operating grace, while the remission of the debt of temporal punishment belongs to co-operating grace, in so far as man, by bearing punishment patiently with the help of Divine grace, is released also from the debt of temporal punishment."

Ibid., Q. LXXXVI, Art. IV.

n. "... Every prayer has the character of satisfaction, for though it be sweet to the soul it is painful to the body."

Ibid., Supp. Part Three, Book Four, Q. XV, Art. III.

7. Indulgences

a. "Satisfactory punishment has a twofold purpose, viz., to pay the debt, and to serve as a remedy for the avoidance of sin. Accordingly, as a remedy against future sin, the satisfaction of one does not profit another, for the flesh of one man cannot be tamed by another's fast; nor does one man acquire the habit of well-doing through the actions of another, except accidentally, in so far as a man, by his good actions, may merit an increase of grace for another, since grace is the most efficacious remedy for the avoidance of sin. But this is by way of merit rather than of satisfaction. On the other hand, AS REGARDS THE PAYMENT OF THE DEBT, ONE MAN CAN SATISFY FOR ANOTHER, PROVIDED HE BE IN A STATE OF CHARITY, so that his works may avail for satisfaction. Nor is it necessary that he who satisfies for another should undergo a greater punishment than the principal would have to undergo (as some maintain, who argue that a man profits more by his own punishment than by another's), because punishment derives its power of satisfaction chiefly from charity whereby man bears it. And since greater charity is evidenced by a man satisfying for another than for himself, less punishment is required of him who satisfies for another, than of the principal. . . . "

Ibid., Q. XIII, Art. II.

b. "Now one man can satisfy for another, as we have explained above (Q. XIII, A. II). And the saints, in whom this superabundance of satisfactions is found, did not perform their good works for this or that particular person, who needs the remission of his punishment (else he would have received the remission without any indulgence at all), BUT THEY PERFORMED THEM FOR THE WHOLE CHURCH IN GENERAL, EVEN AS THE APOSTLE DECLARES THAT HE FILLS UP THOSE THINGS THAT ARE WANTING OF THE SUFFERINGS OF CHRIST . . . FOR HIS BODY, WHICH IS THE CHURCH to whom he wrote (Colossians 1:24). THESE MERITS, THEN, ARE THE COMMON PROPERTY OF THE WHOLE CHURCH. Now those things which are the common property of a number are distributed to the various individuals according to the judgment of him who rules them all. Hence, just as one man would obtain the remission of his punishment if another were to satisfy for him, so would he too if another's satisfactions be applied to him by one who has the power to do so."

Ibid., Q. XXV, Art. I.

c. " . . . True contrition and confession are demanded as conditions for gaining all indulgences."

Ibid., Q. XXVII, Art. I.

8. The Holy Eucharist

a. "Just as for the spiritual life there had to be Baptism, which is spiritual
   generation; and Confirmation, which is spiritual growth: so there needed
   to be the Sacrament of the Eucharist, WHICH IS SPIRITUAL FOOD.
   Ibid., Part Three, Third Number, Q. LXXIII, Art. I.

b. "The reception of Baptism is necessary for starting the spiritual life,
   while the receiving of the Eucharist is requisite for its consummation."
   Ibid., Art. III.

c. "As Baptism is called the sacrament of faith, which is the foundation
   of the spiritual life, so THE EUCHARIST IS TERMED THE SACRA-
   MENT OF CHARITY, which is the bond of perfection (Colossians
   3:14)."
   Ibid.

d. "The presence of Christ's true body and blood in this sacrament cannot
   be detected by sense, nor understanding, but by faith alone, which rests
   upon Divine authority. Hence, on Luke 22:19, 'This is My body,
   which shall be delivered up for you,' Cyril says: 'Doubt not whether
   this be true; but take rather the Saviour's words with faith; for since
   He is the Truth, He lieth not.' "
   Ibid., Q. LXXV, Art. I.

e. "I answer that, after what we have said above (A. I), IT MUST BE
   HELD MOST CERTAINLY THAT THE WHOLE CHRIST IS
   UNDER EACH SACRAMENTAL SPECIES YET NOT ALIKE IN
   EACH. For the body of Christ is indeed present under the species of
   bread by the power of the sacrament, while the blood is there from real
   concomitance, as stated above (A. I ad I) in regard to the soul and Godhead of Christ; and under the species of wine the blood is present by
   the power of the sacrament, and His body by real concomitance, as is
   also His soul and Godhead: because now Christ's blood is not separated
   from His body, as it was at the time of His Passion and death."
   Ibid., Q. LXXVI, Art. II.

f. In this place we are taught the Sacrament of Communion. For he who
   eats and drinks the Flesh and Blood of the Lord, abides in the Lord
   Himself and the Lord in him. For there is a new sort of commingling
   and one beyond understanding that God is in us and we in God. . . .
   Cyril declares (Lib. 10, c. 13) that Christ is in us 'not only through
   the indwelling, which is meant by love, BUT ALSO BY A PARTICI-
   PATION OF NATURE.' Cyril of Jerusalem (Cat. 4 Mystag.) declares
   that in Holy Communion we become Christ-bearers, yea, concorporate
   and united by consanguinity with Christ."
   Cornelius à Lapide (St. John 6:57).

g. "St. Chrysostom ('Hom. 61 ad Pop.') teaches that WE IN THE EUCHARIST ARE UNITED AND COMMINGLED WITH THE FLESH OF CHRIST, not only by love and consent of will, but also really and substantially. 'Wherefore,' saith he, 'He hath commingled Himself with us, and united His Body to ours, that we should be made one whole, even as a body is connected with its head.' "

Ibid. (6:56).

h. "St. Cyril . . . says: 'Because the Flesh of Christ is the Flesh of God, which is united to the Word of God, Who is by His nature Life, and thus is made life-giving; the Eucharist therefore quickens the soul, because It preserves, feeds, augments grace. Also It blots out venial sins, and even mortal sins, if a man has forgotten them. And It will raise up the body from death.' "

Ibid. (6:55).

i. "Innocent III says ('De S. Alt. Myst.,' iv) that this sacrament blots out venial sins, and wards off mortal sins."

St. Thomas Aquinas, loc. cit., Q. LXXIX, Art. IV.

j. "So St. Augustine is explained after his manner by his disciple St. Bernard ('Serm. 3 in Ps. XC') : 'What is it to eat His Flesh and drink His Blood but to participate in His sufferings and to imitate His life in the flesh? Wherefore also that spotless Sacrament of the Altar sets this forth, when we receive the Lord's Body. As that form of bread appears to enter into us, so we know by that life which He had upon earth He enters into us to dwell in our hearts by faith.' "

Cornelius à Lapide (St. John 6:52).

k. "I am the living bread [bread is used by a hebraism for FOOD] quickening those who eat Me in Myself Who am Life AND COM-MUNICATING MY LIFE TO THEM."

Ibid. (6:51).

l. " 'If anyone shall eat! For this Bread gives to the soul the life of grace, which endures even to the life of glory for all eternity. AND IT SHALL MAKE THE BODY TO RISE FROM DEATH TO LIVE TOGETHER WITH THE SOUL GLORIOUSLY FOR EVER.' "

Ibid. (6:52).

m. "The Council of Nice calls the Eucharist 'the symbol of the resurrection.' And St. Ignatius calls It the 'medicine of immortality.' St. Cyril in this verse calls It 'good nourishing for immortality and eternal life.' . . . St. Ireneaus, from the truth that we communicate of the Flesh and Blood of an immortal Christ proves the resurrection, that is to say, that we shall rise to life immortal. Suarez [says]: . . . 'The Eucharist therefore is the instrumental cause of the resurrection (a moral, that is, not a physical cause) because of which Christ will cause us to rise again.' "

Ibid. (6:55).

n. "For Christ came down from heaven not as man, but as God. Wherefore he who eateth Him in the Eucharist shall live forever, because in truth he eateth God and the Godhead, WHICH BEING EVER PRESENT WITH HIM WHO EATETH, CONTINUALLY BREATHES INTO HIM HIS OWN LIFE."

Ibid. (6:59).

o. "Since by Christ's Body and Blood the personality of the devout communicant is elevated and ennobled, consecrated and sanctified, Christ cherishes, loves and esteems it, thus to speak, as His own, for it is in a special manner espoused to and possessed by Him. THIS ASPECT GIVES A NEW CLAIM TO THE GLORIFICATION OF THE BODY AT THE GENERAL RESURRECTION; for also in the worthy reception of the glorified Body there lies a reason for the Lord to 'reform the body of our lowness and make it like to the body of His glory' (Philippians 3:21). The eternal glorification of the body is, consequently, already here below prepared and established through the cure and sanctification imparted to mortal flesh by the heavenly Eucharistic Food."

Gihr, op. cit., p. 733.

p. "St. Cyril says the body of Christ quickens, and by our participation of it restores us to incorruption. FOR IT IS THE BODY OF NONE OTHER THAN OF THE LIFE ITSELF."

Cornelius à Lapide (St. John 6:59).

q. "This sacrament is both a SACRIFICE and a SACRAMENT; it has the nature of a sacrifice inasmuch as it is offered up; and it has the nature of a sacrament inasmuch as it is received. And therefore it has the effect of a sacrament in the recipient, and the effect of a sacrifice in the offerer, or in them for whom it is offered."

St. Thomas Aquinas, loc. cit., Art. V.

r. "... This sacrament is not only a sacrament, but also a sacrifice. For it has the nature of a sacrifice inasmuch as in this sacrament Christ's Passion is represented, whereby 'Christ offered Himself a Victim to God' (Ephesians 5:2); and it has the nature of a sacrament inasmuch as invisible grace is bestowed in this sacrament under a visible species...."

Ibid., Art. VII.

s. "It is manifest that the Sacrament of Order is ordained to the consecration of the Eucharist: and the Sacrament of Baptism to the reception of the Eucharist: while a man is perfected by Confirmation, so as not to fear to abstain from this sacrament. By Penance and Extreme Unction man is prepared to receive the Body of Christ worthily. And Matrimony, at least in its signification, touches this sacrament; in so far as it signifies the union of Christ with the Church."

Ibid., Q. LXV, Art. III.

t. "ABSOLUTELY SPEAKING, THE SACRAMENT OF THE EUCHARIST IS THE GREATEST OF ALL THE SACRAMENTS: and this may be shown in three ways. First of all because it contains Christ Himself substantially: whereas the other sacraments contain a certain instrumental power which is a share of Christ's power."

Ibid.

u. "Augustine (Paschasius) says ('De Corp. Dom.,' xii): 'Within the Catholic Church, in the mystery of the Lord's Body and Blood, nothing greater is done by a good priest, nothing less by an evil priest, BECAUSE IT IS NOT BY THE MERITS OF THE CONSECRATOR THAT THE SACRAMENT IS ACCOMPLISHED, but by the Creator's word, and by the power of the Holy Spirit.'"

Ibid., Q. LXXXII, Art. V.

v. "There are two ways of receiving this sacrament, namely, spiritually and sacramentally. Now it is clear that all are bound to eat it at least spiritually, because this is to be incorporated in Christ, as was said above (Q. LXXIII, A. 3 ad I). Now spiritual eating comprises the desire or yearning for receiving this sacrament, as was said above (A. I ad 3, A. 2). Therefore, a man cannot be saved without desiring to receive this sacrament. Now a desire would be vain except it were fulfilled when opportunity presented itself. CONSEQUENTLY, IT IS EVIDENT THAT A MAN IS BOUND TO RECEIVE THIS SACRAMENT, NOT ONLY BY VIRTUE OF THE CHURCH'S PRECEPT, BUT ALSO BY VIRTUE OF THE LORD'S COMMAND (Luke 22: 19): 'Do this in memory of Me.' But by the precept of the Church there are fixed times for fulfilling Christ's commands."

Ibid., Q. LXXX, Art. XI.

9. Extreme Unction

a. "Each sacrament was instituted for the purpose of one principal effect, though it may, in consequence, produce other effects besides. And since a sacrament causes what it signifies, the principal effect of a sacrament must be gathered from its signification. Now this sacrament is conferred by way of a kind of medicament, even as Baptism is conferred by way of washing, and the purpose of a medicament is to expel sickness. HENCE THE CHIEF OBJECT OF THE INSTITUTION OF THIS SACRAMENT IS TO CURE THE SICKNESS OF SIN. Therefore, just as Baptism is a spiritual regeneration, and Penance a spiritual resurrection, so Extreme Unction is a spiritual healing or cure."

Ibid., Supp. Part Three, Book Four, Q. XXX, Art. I.

b. "This sacrament is the last remedy that the Church can give, since it is an immediate preparation for glory."

Ibid., Q. XXXII, Art. II.

c. "Our Lord did and said many things which are not related in the Gospel. For the Evangelists were intent on handing down chiefly those things that were necessary for salvation or concerned the building of the ecclesiastical edifice. Hence they related the institution by Christ of Baptism, Penance, the Eucharist and Orders, rather than of Extreme Unction and Confirmation, which are not necessary for salvation, nor do they concern the building or division of the Church. As a matter of fact, however, an anointing done by the Apostles is mentioned in the Gospel (Mark 6:13) where it is said that they anointed the sick with oil."

Ibid., Q. XXIX, Art. III.

d. "Extreme Unction does not cause a bodily healing by a natural property of the matter, but by the Divine power which works reasonably. And since reasonable working never produces a secondary effect, except in so far as it is required for the principal effect, it follows that a bodily healing does not always ensue from this sacrament, but only when it is requisite for the spiritual healing: and then it produces it always, provided there be no obstacles on the part of the recipient."

Ibid., Q. XXX, Art. II.

10. Matrimony

a. "Before sin matrimony was instituted by God, when He fashioned a helpmate for man out of his rib, and said to them: Increase and multiply."

Ibid., Supp. Part Three, Q. XLII, Art. II.

b. "In marriage there is a contract whereby one is bound to pay the other the marital debt: wherefore just as in other contracts, the bond is unfitting if a person bind himself to what he cannot give or do, so the marriage contract is unfitting, if it be made by one who cannot pay the marital debt."

Ibid., Q. LVIII, Art. I.

c. "The marriage act is always either sinful or meritorious in one who is in a state of grace. For if the motive of the marriage act be a virtue, whether of justice that they may render the debt, or of religion, that they may beget children for the worship of God, it is meritorious."

Ibid., Q. XLI, Art. IV.

d. "Matrimony, according to the general opinion of theologians, is defined: The conjugal union of man and woman, contracted between two qualified persons, which obliges them to live together throughout life.

"In order that the different parts of this definition may be better understood, it should be taught that, although a perfect marriage has all the following conditions — namely, internal consent, external compact expressed by words, the obligation and tie which arise from the contract, and the marriage debt by which it is consummated; — yet the obligation and tie expressed by the word UNION alone have the force and nature of marriage.

"The special character of this union is marked by the word CONJUGAL.

"Next follow the words BETWEEN QUALIFIED PERSONS: for persons excluded by law cannot contract marriage, and if they do, their marriage is invalid. . . .

"It is necessary that the consent be expressed in words denoting present time. Marriage is not a mere donation, but a mutual agreement; and therefore the consent of one of the parties is insufficient for marriage, while the mutual consent of both is essential."

Catechism of the Council of Trent.

e. "The chief good of marriage is the offspring to be brought up to the worship of God. Now since education is the work of father and mother in common, each of them intends to bring up the child to the worship of God according to their own faith. Consequently if they be of different faith, the intention of one will be contrary to the intention of the other, and therefore there cannot be a fitting marriage between them. For this reason disparity of faith previous to marriage is an impediment to the marriage contract."

St. Thomas Aquinas, loc. cit., Q. LIX, Art. I.

11. Holy Orders

a. "Wherefore that this beauty might not be lacking to the Church, He [Jesus] established Order in her so that some should deliver the sacraments to others, being thus made like to God in their own way, as co-operating with God; even as in the natural body, some members act on others."

Ibid., Q. XXXIV, Art. I.

b. "A priest represents Christ in that He fulfilled a certain ministry by Himself, whereas a bishop represents Him in that He instituted other ministers and founded the Church. Hence it belongs to a bishop to dedicate a thing to the Divine offices, as establishing the Divine worship after the manner of Christ. For this reason also a bishop is especially called the bridegroom of the Church, even as Christ is."

Ibid., Q. XL, Art. IV.

c. " ... It belongs to a bishop to assign others to places in all the Divine services. Hence he alone confirms, because those who are confirmed receive the office, as it were, of confessing the Faith; (again, he alone blesses virgins, who are images of the Church, Christ's spouse, the care of which is entrusted chiefly to him) ; and he it is who consecrates the candidates to the ministry of Orders, and, by his consecration, appoints the vessels that they are to use."

Ibid., Q. XXXVIII, Art. I.

d. "The bishop in conferring Orders does two things: for he prepares the candidates for the reception of Orders, and delivers to them the power of Order. He prepares them both by instructing them in their respective offices, and by doing something to them, so that they may be adapted to receive the power. This preparation consists of three things, namely blessing, imposition of hands and anointing. By the blessing they are enlisted in the Divine service, wherefore the blessing is given to all. By the imposition of hands the fulness of grace is given, whereby they are qualified for exalted duties; wherefore only deacons and priests receive the imposition of hands, because they are competent to dispense the sacraments, although the latter as principal dispensers, the former as ministers. But by the anointing they are consecrated for the purpose of handling the sacrament, wherefore the anointing is done to the priests alone who touch the Body of Christ with their own hands; even as a chalice is anointed because it holds the Blood, and the paten because it holds the Body.

"The conferring of power is effected by giving them something pertaining to their proper act. And since the principal act of a priest is to consecrate the Body and Blood of Christ, the priestly character is imprinted at the very giving of the chalice under the prescribed form of words."

Ibid., Q. XXXVII, Art. V.

e. "It is at least required that the ordainer know that nothing contrary to holiness is in the candidate for ordination. But besides this he is required to take the greatest care, in proportion to the Order or office to be enjoined, ... so as to be certain of the qualifications of those to be promoted, at least from the testification of others. This is the meaning of the Apostle when he says (1 Timothy 5:22): 'IMPOSE NOT HANDS LIGHTLY ON ANY MAN.'"

Ibid., Q. XXXVI, Art. IV.

f. "... Holiness of life is requisite for Orders, as a matter of precept, but not as essential to the sacrament; and if a wicked man be ordained, he receives the Order none the less, and yet with sin withal.

"... Just as the sinner dispenses sacraments validly so does he receive validly the sacrament of Orders, and as he dispenses unworthily, even so he receives unworthily."

Ibid., Art. I.

g. "Wherefore whoever fulfils unworthily the duties of his Order follows unjustly after that which is just, and acts contrary to a precept of the law, and thereby sins mortally."

Ibid., Art. V.

h. "By a certain fittingness the very nature of Holy Order requires that it should be an impediment to marriage: because those who are in Holy Orders handle the sacred vessels and the sacraments; (wherefore it is becoming that they keep their bodies clean by continence — Isaias 52:11). But it is owing to the Church's ordinance that it is actually an impediment to marriage."

Ibid., Q. LIII, Art. III.

i. "No one can receive what he has not the power to receive. Now the character of Baptism gives a man the power to receive the other sacraments. Wherefore he that has not the baptismal character, can receive no other sacrament; and consequently the character of Order presupposes the character of Baptism."

Ibid., Q. XXXV, Art. III.

j. "Although in Baptism there is conferred a spiritual power to receive the other sacraments, for which reason it imprints a character, nevertheless this is not its principal effect, but the inward cleansing; wherefore Baptism would be given even though the former motive did not exist. On the other hand, Order denotes power principally. Wherefore the character which is a spiritual power is included in the definition of Order, but not in that of Baptism."

Ibid., Q. XXXIV, Art. II.

k. "For all that a man may return to the laity, the character always remains in him. This is evident from the fact that if he return to the clerical state, he does not again receive the Order which he had already."

Ibid., Q. XXXV, Art. II.

l. "The bishop gives the priestly power of Order, not as though coming from himself, but instrumentally, as God's minister, and its effect cannot be taken away by man. ... And therefore the bishop cannot take this power away, just as neither can he who baptizes take away the baptismal character."

Ibid., Part Three, Third Number, Q. LXXXII, Art. VIII.

F. BIBLICAL BACKGROUND

Pope Pius VI expresses his wishes concerning the reading of Holy Scripture by the laity in the following words: "...You judge exceedingly well that the faithful should be excited to the reading of the Holy Scriptures: for these are the most abundant sources, which ought to be left open to everyone, to draw from them purity of morals and of doctrine, to eradicate the errors which are so widely disseminated in these corrupt times."

The following are excerpts from Holy Scripture concerning the Sacraments. By studying these excerpts a teacher will be drawing from "the most abundant sources."

1. God Wants Me Holy

a. Exodus 20:5, 6

"I am the Lord thy God, ... showing mercy unto thousands to them that love Me and keep My commandments."

b. Leviticus 26:3, 11, 12

"If you walk in My precepts, and keep My commandments, and do them, ... I will set My tabernacle in the midst of you, and My soul shall not cast you off. I WILL WALK AMONG YOU, AND WILL BE YOUR GOD, AND YOU SHALL BE MY PEOPLE."

Leviticus 26:14, 15, 17, 19, 24

"... If you despise My laws, and contemn My judgments, so as not to do those things which are appointed by Me, and to make void My covenant; ... I will set My face against you, and you shall fall down before your enemies, and shall be made subject to them that hate you, and you shall flee when no man pursueth you. ... And I will break the pride of your stubbornness, and I will make to you the heaven above as iron, and the earth as brass. ... I also will walk contrary to you, and will strike you seven times for your sins."

c. Deuteronomy 4:5, 6

"... For this is your wisdom and understanding in the sight of nations, that hearing all these precepts, they may say: Behold a wise and understanding people, a great nation."

Deuteronomy 4:40

"Keep His precepts and commandments, which I command thee: THAT IT MAY BE WELL WITH THEE, and thou mayest remain a long time upon the land which the Lord thy God will give thee."

Deuteronomy 6:25

"AND HE WILL BE MERCIFUL TO US, if we keep and do all His precepts before the Lord our God as He hath commanded us."

Deuteronomy 10:12, 13

"And now, Israel, what doth the Lord thy God require of thee, but that thou fear the Lord thy God, and walk in His ways, and love Him, and serve the Lord thy God with all thy heart and with all thy soul: and keep the commandments of the Lord, ... which I command this day, THAT IT MAY BE WELL WITH THEE?"

d. Josue 1:8

"Let not the book of this law depart from thy mouth: but thou shalt meditate on it day and night, that thou mayest observe and do all things that are written in it: then thou shalt direct thy way and understand it."

e. 2 Paralipomenon 24:20

" ... Thus saith the Lord God: Why transgress you the commandment of the Lord, which will not be for your good, and have forsaken the Lord, to make Him forsake you?"

f. Psalm 1:1, 2

"BLESSED IS THE MAN WHO HATH NOT WALKED IN THE COUNSEL OF THE UNGODLY, nor stood in the way of sinners.... But his will is in the law of the Lord, and on His law he shall meditate day and night."

Psalm 102:17, 18

"BUT THE MERCY OF THE LORD IS FROM ETERNITY AND UNTO ETERNITY UPON THEM THAT FEAR HIM: and His justice unto children's children to such as keep His covenant, and are mindful of His commandments to do them."

Psalm 118:4-6

"Thou hast commanded Thy commandments to be kept most diligently. Oh that my ways may be directed to keep Thy justifications! ... THEN SHALL I NOT BE CONFOUNDED, when I shall look into all Thy commandments."

Psalm 118:21

" ... They are cursed who decline from Thy commandments."

Psalm 118:47, 48

"I meditated also on Thy commandments, which I loved. And I lifted up my hands to Thy commandments, which I loved: and I was exercised in Thy justifications."

Psalm 118:92, 93

"Unless Thy law had been my meditation, I had then perhaps perished in my abjection. Thy justifications I will never forget: FOR BY THEM THOU HAST GIVEN ME LIFE."

Psalm 118:98, 100, 104

"...THROUGH THY COMMANDMENT, THOU HAST MADE ME WISER THAN MY ENEMIES: for it is ever with me. ...I have had understanding above ancients: because I have sought Thy commandments....By Thy commandments I have had understanding: therefore have I hated every way of iniquity."

Psalm 118:165

"MUCH PEACE HAVE THEY THAT LOVE THY LAW, and to them there is no stumbling block."

g. Proverbs 29:18

"...HE THAT KEEPETH THE LAW IS BLESSED."

h. Ecclesiastes 8:5

"He that keepeth the commandment, shall find no evil...."

Ecclesiates 9:18

"BETTER IS WISDOM THAN WEAPONS OF WAR: and he that shall offend in one, shall lose many good things."

Ecclesiastes 12:13

"...Fear God, and keep His commandments: for this is all man."

i. Ecclesiasticus 2:12

"For who hath continued in His commandment, and hath been forsaken? or who hath called upon Him, and He despised him?"

Ecclesiasticus 2:18, 21

"They that fear the Lord keep His commandments, and will have patience even until His visitation...."

Ecclesiasticus 10:23

"THAT SEED OF MEN SHALL BE HONORED, WHICH FEAR.ETH GOD: but that seed shall be dishonored which transgresseth the commandments of the Lord."

Ecclesiasticus 17:1, 5, 9

"God created man of the earth, and made him after His own image....He gave them counsel,...and He filled them with the knowledge of understanding....Moreover He gave them instructions, and the law of life for an inheritance."

Ecclesiasticus 23:37

"And they that remain shall know...that there is nothing sweeter than to have regard to the commandments of the Lord."

Ecclesiasticus 26:24

"AS EVERLASTING FOUNDATIONS UPON A SOLID ROCK, so the commandments of God in the heart of a holy woman."

Ecclesiasticus 29:14

"Place thy treasure in the commandments of the most High, AND IT SHALL BRING THEE MORE PROFIT THAN GOLD."

Ecclesiasticus 35:1, 2

". . . It is a wholesome sacrifice to take heed to the commandments, and to depart from all iniquity."

j. Isaias 48:18

"O that thou hadst hearkened to My commandments: thy peace had been as a river, and thy justice as the waves of the sea."

k. Baruch 3:9

"Hear, O Israel, the commandments of life: give ear, THAT THOU MAYEST LEARN WISDOM."

Baruch 4:1

"This is the book of the commandments of God, and the law, that is forever: ALL THEY THAT KEEP IT, SHALL COME TO LIFE: but they that have forsaken it, to death."

l. Ezechiel 20:11

"And I gave them My statutes, and I showed them My judgments, which if a man do, he shall live in them."

m. Matthew 19:16, 17

". . . IF THOU WILT ENTER INTO LIFE, keep the commandments."

n. John 12:49, 50

"For I have not spoken of Myself; but the Father who sent Me, He gave Me commandment what I should say, and what I should speak. AND I KNOW THAT HIS COMMANDMENT IS LIFE EVERLASTING."

John 13:17

"If you know these things, YOU SHALL BE BLESSED if you do them."

John 14:21, 23

"He that hath My commandments, and keepeth them, he it is that loveth Me . . . and MY FATHER WILL LOVE HIM, and We will come to him, and will make Our abode with him."

John 15:10, 14

"If you keep My commandments, you shall abide in My love; as I also have kept My Father's commandments, and do abide in His love.... YOU ARE MY FRIENDS, if you do the things that I command you."

o. Romans 7:12

"Wherefore the law indeed is holy, and the commandment holy, and just, and good."

Romans 12:9-11

"Let love be without dissimulation. Hating that which is evil, cleaving to that which is good.

"Loving one another, ... serving the Lord."

p. Thessalonians 4:3-5, 7, 8

"For this is the will of God, your sanctification: that you should abstain from fornication; that every one of you should know how to possess his vessel in sanctification and honor: not in the passion of lust, like the Gentiles that know not God.... For God hath not called us unto uncleanness, but unto sanctification. Therefore he that despiseth these things, despiseth not man, but God Who also hath given His Holy Spirit in us."

q. I Peter 2:21

"For unto this are you called: because Christ also suffered for us, leaving you an example that you should follow His steps."

I Peter 3:8, 9

"And in fine, be ye all of one mind, having compassion one of another, being lovers of the brotherhood, merciful, modest, humble: not rendering evil for evil, nor railing for railing, but contrariwise, blessing. For unto this you are called, that you may inherit a blessing."

r. I John 2:3-5

"And by this we know that we have known Him, if we keep His commandments. He who saith that he knoweth Him and keepeth not His commandments, is a liar, and the truth is not in him. But he that keepeth His word, IN HIM IN VERY DEED THE CHARITY OF GOD IS PERFECTED: and by this we know that we are in Him."

I John 5:3

"FOR THIS IS THE CHARITY OF GOD, that we keep His commandments: and His commandments are not heavy."

s. 2 John 1:6

"AND THIS IS CHARITY that we walk according to His commandments...."

2. Sin

a. Deuteronomy 11:26, 28

"Behold I set forth in your sight this day a blessing and a curse: A BLESSING, IF YOU OBEY THE COMMANDMENTS of the Lord your God, which I command you this day ... a curse, if you obey not the commandments of the Lord your God, but revolt from the way which now I show you, and walk after strange gods which you know not."

Deuteronomy 30:15

"Consider that I have set before thee this day life and good, and on the other hand death and evil."

Deuteronomy 30:19, 20

"I call heaven and earth to witness this day, that I have set before you life and death, blessing and cursing. CHOOSE THEREFORE LIFE, THAT BOTH THOU AND THY SEED MAY LIVE.... And that thou mayest love the Lord thy God, and obey His voice and adhere to Him (for He is thy life, and the length of thy days)...."

b. Proverbs 14:19

"The evil shall fall down before the good: and the wicked before the gates of the just."

c. Ecclesiasticus 15:14, 17, 18

"... Before man is life and death, good and evil, that which he shall choose shall be given him...."

d. Ecclesiasticus 33:15

"Good is set against evil, and life against death: so also is the sinner against a just man."

e. Jeremias 21:8

"... Thus saith the Lord: BEHOLD I HAVE SET BEFORE YOU THE WAY OF LIFE and the way of death."

f. Amos 5:14, 15

"Seek ye good and not evil.... Hate evil and love good...."

g. Matthew 6:24

"No man can serve two masters. For either he will hate the one, and love the other: or he will sustain the one and despise the other. You cannot serve God and mammon."

3. Baptism

a. Matthew 28:18, 19
"... All power is given to Me in heaven and in earth. Going therefore teach ye all nations; baptizing them...."

b. Mark 16:15, 16
"... He that believeth and is baptized, shall be saved: but he that believeth not shall be condemned."

c. John 3:3-7
"... Jesus answered: Amen, amen, I say to thee, unless a man be born again of water and the Holy Ghost, he cannot enter into the kingdom of God...."

d. Acts 2:37, 41
"... Peter said to them: Do penance and be baptized every one of you...."

Acts 8:36-38
"... And they went down into the water, both Philip and the eunuch; and he baptized him."

Acts 10:47, 48
"... And he [Peter] commanded them to be baptized in the name of the Lord Jesus Christ."

Acts 18:8
"... And many of the Corinthians hearing, believed, and were baptized."

Acts 19:1-5
"... Having heard these things, they were baptized in the name of the Lord Jesus."

Acts 22:16
"... Rise up, and be baptized, and wash away thy sins...."

e. Galatians 3:26, 27
"... For as many of you as have been baptized in Christ, have put on Christ."

f. Ephesians 4:1-5
"... ONE LORD, ONE FAITH, ONE BAPTISM."

g. Titus 3:5
"... But according to His mercy, he saved us by the laver of regeneration and renovation of the Holy Ghost...."

4. Temples of the Living God

a. Matthew 10:20

". . . For it is not you that speak but the Spirit of your Father that speaketh in you."

b. John 14:17, 23

"The Spirit of Truth, Whom the world cannot receive, . . . but you shall know Him; because He shall abide with you, and shall be in you. . . .

"If any one love Me, he will keep My word, and My Father will love him, and We will come to him, and will make Our abode with him."

c. Romans 8:14-16

"For whosoever are led by the Spirit of God, they are the sons of God.

"FOR THE SPIRIT HIMSELF GIVETH TESTIMONY TO OUR SPIRIT, that we are the sons of God."

d. I Corinthians 3:16, 17

"Know you not, that YOU ARE THE TEMPLE OF GOD, and that the Spirit of God dwelleth in you?

"But if any man violate the temple of God, him shall God destroy. For the temple of God is holy which you are."

I Corinthians 6:19, 20

". . . KNOW YOU NOT THAT YOUR MEMBERS ARE THE TEMPLE OF THE HOLY GHOST, WHO IS IN YOU, Whom you have from God, and you are not your own? For you are bought with a great price. Glorify and bear God in your body."

I Corinthians 12:13

"FOR IN ONE SPIRIT WERE WE ALL BAPTIZED INTO ONE BODY, whether Jews or Gentiles, whether bond or free; and in one Spirit we have all been made to drink."

e. 2 Corinthians 6:16

"FOR YOU ARE THE TEMPLE OF THE LIVING GOD; as God saith: I will dwell in them, and walk among them: and I will be their God, and they shall be My people."

f. Galatians 4:4-7

"And because you are sons, GOD HATH SENT THE SPIRIT OF HIS SON INTO YOUR HEARTS, crying: Abba, Father. . . . Therefore now he is not a servant, but a son.

"And if a son, an heir also through God."

5. Confirmation

a. Acts 2:1-5

"And when the days of the Pentecost were accomplished, they were all together in one place: and suddenly there came a sound from heaven, as of a mighty wind coming, and it filled the whole house where they were sitting; and there appeared to them parted tongues as it were of fire, and it sat upon every one of them.

"AND THEY WERE ALL FILLED WITH THE HOLY GHOST."

Acts 8:14-19

"Now when the Apostles . . . had heard that Samaria had received the word of God, they sent unto them Peter and John. . . .

"THEN THEY LAID THEIR HANDS UPON THEM AND THEY RECEIVED THE HOLY GHOST. . . . And when Simon saw that BY THE IMPOSITION OF THE HANDS OF THE APOSTLES, THE HOLY GHOST WAS GIVEN. . . ."

Acts 19:1-6

". . . AND WHEN PAUL HAD IMPOSED HIS HANDS ON THEM, THE HOLY GHOST CAME UPON THEM."

b. 2 Corinthians 1:21, 22

"Now He that confirmeth us with you in Christ, and that hath anointed us, is God, Who also hath sealed us; and given the pledge of the Spirit in our hearts."

c. Ephesians 1:13

"In Whom (Christ) you also, after you had heard the word of truth, . . . in Whom also believing, you were signed with the Holy Spirit of promise."

d. Titus 3:5

"Not by the works of justice which we have done, but according to His mercy, He saved us, by the laver of regeneration, and renovation of the Holy Ghost."

e. 1 John 2:20, 27

"But you have the unction from the Holy One, and know all things. . . .

"And as for you, let the unction, which you have received from Him, abide in you. And you have no need that any man teach you; but as His unction teacheth you all things, and is truth, and is no lie. And as it hath taught you, abide in Him."

6. Good Angels

a. Genesis 19:1, 12, 13

"And the two angels came to Sodom in the evening . . . and they said to Lot. . . . We will destroy this place. . . ."

Genesis 22:9-12

". . . And behold an angel of the Lord from heaven called to him. . . ."

b. Exodus 32:34

"But go thou, and lead this people whither I have told thee: my angel shall go before thee."

c. Tobias 12:1-3, 17-20

". . . And the angel said to them: Peace be to you, fear not. . . . For when I was with you, I was there by the will of God. . . ."

d. Judith 13:20

"But as the same Lord liveth, His angel hath been my keeper. . . ."

e. Psalm 33:8

"The angel of the Lord shall . . . deliver them."

Psalm 90:11, 12

"For He hath given His angels charge over thee to keep thee in all thy ways. . . ."

Psalm 96:7

"Adore Him, all you His angels."

f. Daniel 7: 9, 10

". . . Thousands of thousands ministered unto Him. . . ."

Daniel 12:1

"But at that time shall Michael rise up, the great prince who standeth for the children of thy people. . . . And at that time shall thy people be saved every one that shall be found written in the book."

Daniel 14:32-38

". . . And Daniel arose and ate. And the angel of the Lord presently set Habacuc again in his own place."

g. Matthew 1:20

". . . Behold the angel of the Lord appeared to him [Joseph] in his sleep. . . ."

Matthew 2:13

"And after they [the wise men] were departed, behold an angel of the Lord appeared in sleep to Joseph. . . ."

Matthew 2:19, 20

" . . . An angel of the Lord appeared . . . to Joseph in Egypt. . . . "

Matthew 13:41, 42, 49, 50

"The Son of Man shall send His angels. . . . The angels shall go out, and shall separate the wicked from among the just. . . ."

Matthew 18:10

" . . . For I say to you that their angels in heaven always see the face of My Father Who is in heaven."

Matthew 24:31

"And he shall send His angels . . . and they shall gather together His elect from the four winds."

Matthew 28:1-3, 5-7

" . . . For an angel of the Lord descended from heaven, and coming, rolled back the stone, and sat upon it. . . ."

h. **Luke 1:11-13, 18, 19**

" . . . But the angel said to him: Fear not, Zachary."

Luke 1:26-28, 31-35

" . . . In the sixth month the angel Gabriel was sent from God . . . to a virgin espoused to a man whose name was Joseph. . . ."

Luke 2:8-14

" . . . And suddenly there was with the angel a multitude of the heavenly army, praising God and saying: Glory to God in the highest. . . ."

Luke 15:10

"So I say to you, there shall be joy before the angels of God upon one sinner doing penance."

Luke 22:41-43

" . . . And there appeared to Him an angel from heaven, strengthening Him."

i. **John 20:11-13**

"And she saw two angels in white, sitting, one at the head and one at the feet, where the body of Jesus had been laid. . . ."

j. **Acts 5:18-23**

" . . . But an angel of the Lord by night opening the doors of the prison and leading them. . . ."

Acts 27:22-24

". . . For an angel of God . . . stood by me this night, saying: Fear not, Paul. . . ."

k. Colossians 1:16

". . . Whether thrones, or dominations or principalities, or powers: all things were created by Him and in Him."

l. Hebrews 1:14

"Are they not all ministering spirits . . . ?"

m. Apocalypse 5:11

". . . And I heard the voice of many angels round about the throne. . . ."

Apocalypse 12:7, 8

"And there was a great battle in heaven, Michael and his angels fought with the dragon, and the dragon fought and his angels. And they prevailed not, neither was their place found any more in heaven."

7. Bad Angels

a. Job 4:18

". . . In His angels He found wickedness."

b. Wisdom 2:23-25

". . . By the envy of the devil, death came into the world."

c. Isaias 14:12-15

"How art thou fallen from heaven, O Lucifer. . . . But yet thou shalt be brought down to hell, into the depth of the pit."

d. Matthew 17:17-20

"And Jesus rebuked him, and the devil went out of him and the child was cured from that hour."

e. Luke 8:5-12

". . . And they by the wayside are they that hear; then the devil cometh, and taketh the word out of their heart, lest believing they should be saved."

Luke 10:18

". . . I saw Satan like lightning falling from heaven."

f. John 8:44

"He stood not in the truth; because the truth is not in him."

g. 2 Corinthians 2:11

"... That we be not overreached by Satan. For we are not ignorant of his devices."

2 Corinthians 10:3-5

"For though we walk in the flesh we do not war according to the flesh. For the weapons of our warfare are not carnal, but mighty to God, unto the pulling down of fortifications, destroying counsels."

2 Corinthians 11:14

"For Satan himself transformeth himself into an angel of light."

h. Ephesians 4:27

"Give not place to the devil."

Ephesians 6:11-13, 16

"Put you on the armor of God that you may be able to stand against the deceits of the devil. For our wrestling is not against flesh and blood; but against principalities and powers, against the rulers of the world of this darkness, against the spirits of wickedness in the high places. ...."

i. James 2:19

"Thou believest that there is one God. Thou dost well: the devils also believe and tremble."

James 4:7

"Be subject therefore to God, but resist the devil and he will fly from you."

j. 1 Peter 5:8, 9

"Be sober and watch: because your adversary the devil, as a roaring lion, goeth about, seeking whom he may devour. Whom resist ye strong in faith. ...."

k. 2 Peter 2:4

"For if God spared not the angels that sinned, but delivered them, drawn down by infernal ropes to the lower hell, unto torments, to be reserved unto judgment."

l. 1 John 3:8

"He that committeth sin is of the devil, for the devil sinneth from the beginning. For this purpose the Son of God appeared, that He might destroy the works of the devil."

m. Jude 1:6

"And the angels who kept not their principality, but forsook their own habitation, He hath reserved unto darkness in everlasting chains, unto the judgment of the great day."

8. Penance

a. Matthew 16:18, 19

"... and I will give to thee the keys of the kingdom of heaven.

"And whatsoever thou shalt bind upon earth, it shall be bound also in heaven; and whatsoever thou shalt loose on earth, it shall be loosed also in heaven."

Matthew 18:18

"Amen I say to you, whatsoever you shall bind upon earth, shall be bound also in heaven; and whatsoever you shall loose upon earth, shall be loosed also in heaven."

b. John 20:21-23

"... Peace be to you. As the Father hath sent Me, I also send you.

"When He had said this, He breathed on them; and He said to them: Receive ye the Holy Ghost. Whose sins you shall forgive, they are forgiven them; and whose sins you shall retain, they are retained."

c. Acts 19:11, 17, 18

"And God wrought by the hand of Paul more than common miracles.

"... and the name of the Lord Jesus was magnified.

"And many of them that believed, came confessing and declaring their deeds."

9. Extreme Unction

a. Mark 6:13

"And they (the Apostles) cast out many devils and ANOINTED WITH OIL many that were sick, and healed them."

b. James 5:14, 15

"Is any man sick among you? Let him bring in the priests of the Church and let them pray over him, ANOINTING HIM WITH OIL in the name of the Lord."

10. The Holy Eucharist: Prefigured

a. Genesis 14:18-20

"But MELCHISEDECH, the king of Salem, BRINGING FORTH BREAD AND WINE, for he was the priest of the most high God, ... Said: ... Blessed be the most high God...."

b. Exodus 16:4-15

"And the Lord said to Moses: Behold I will rain bread from heaven for you: ... And Moses said to them: THIS IS THE BREAD WHICH THE LORD HATH GIVEN YOU TO EAT."

c. Leviticus 24:1, 5, 9

"And the Lord spoke to Moses, saying: ... THOU SHALT TAKE ALSO FINE FLOUR, ... BECAUSE IT IS MOST HOLY OF THE SACRIFICES OF THE LORD BY A PERPETUAL RITE."

d. 2 Paralipomenon 6:18

"IS IT CREDIBLE THEN THAT GOD SHOULD DWELL WITH MEN ON THE EARTH? If heaven, and the heavens of heavens do not contain Thee, how much less this house which I have built?"

e. Psalm 77:23-25

"... had rained down manna upon them, to eat, and had given them the bread of heaven. MAN ATE THE BREAD OF ANGELS."

f. Wisdom 16:20

"THOU DIDST FEED THY PEOPLE WITH THE FOOD OF ANGELS, AND GAVEST THEM BREAD FROM HEAVEN...."

g. Ecclesiasticus 24:25-30

"In me is all grace of the way and of the truth, IN ME IS ALL HOPE OF LIFE and of virtue. ... Come over to me, all ye that desire me, and be filled with my fruits. For my spirit is sweet above honey. ... THEY THAT EAT ME ... THEY THAT DRINK ME ... THEY THAT WORK BY ME, shall not sin."

h. Jeremias 31:25

"For I have inebriated the weary soul; and I HAVE FILLED EVERY HUNGRY SOUL."

11.   The Holy Eucharist: Instituted

The following texts from both the Douay and Westminster versions of The New Testament are given under the heading, "The Perpetual Sacrifice of The New Law," Book Four, pages 171, 172.

a. Matthew 26:26-28
b. Mark 14:22-24
c. Luke 22:19, 20
d. I Corinthians 11:23-29

12.   Supersubstantial Bread

a. Matthew 6:11
"Give us this day OUR SUPERSUBSTANTIAL BREAD."

b. Luke 24:30
"And it came to pass, whilst He was at table with them, He took bread, and blessed, and brake, and gave to them."

c. John 6:48-60
"I am the bread of life. . . . I am THE LIVING BREAD which came down from heaven. . . . He that eateth this bread shall live forever. . . .
"These things he said, teaching in the synagogue in Capharnaum."

d. Acts 2:42-46
". . . and they were persevering in the doctrine of the Apostles, and in the communication of the breaking of bread and in prayers. . . . And continuing daily with one accord in the temple, and breaking bread from house to house, they took their meat with gladness and simplicity of heart."

Acts 20:7
"And on the first day of the week when we were assembled to break bread. . . ."

e. I Corinthians 10:16, 17
"THE CHALICE OF BENEDICTION, WHICH WE BLESS, IS IT NOT THE COMMUNION OF THE BLOOD OF CHRIST? AND THE BREAD WHICH WE BREAK, IS IT NOT THE PARTAKING OF THE BODY OF THE LORD? . . ."

f. 2 Corinthians 9:15
"Thanks be to God for HIS UNSPEAKABLE GIFT."

13. Matrimony

a. Matthew 5:31, 32

"... But I say to you, that whosoever shall put away his wife, excepting for the cause of fornication, maketh her to commit adultery; and he that shall marry her that is put away, committeth adultery."

b. Mark 10:2-12

"And the Pharisees coming to Him asked Him: Is it lawful for a man to put away his wife?... To whom Jesus answering said... from the beginning of the creation God made them male and female.

"For this cause a man shall leave his father and mother; and shall cleave to his wife.

"And they two shall be in one flesh.... (see Genesis 2:23, 24).

"What therefore God hath joined together, let not man put asunder...."

c. Luke 16:18

"Every one that putteth away his wife, and marrieth another, committeth adultery; and he that marrieth her that is put away from her husband, committeth adultery."

d. Romans 7:2, 3

"... Therefore, whilst her husband liveth, she shall be called an adulteress, if she be with another man: but if her husband be dead, she is delivered from the law of her husband; so that she is not an adulteress, if she be with another man."

e. I Corinthians 7:10-16

"But to them that are married, not I but the Lord commandeth, that the wife depart not from her husband.

"And if she depart, that she remain unmarried, or be reconciled to her husband. And let not the husband put away his wife...."

I Corinthians 38-40

"Therefore, both he that giveth his virgin in marriage, doth well; and he that giveth her not, doth better.

"A woman is bound by the law as long as her husband liveth; but if her husband die, she is at liberty: let her marry to whom she will; only in the Lord."

f. Ephesians 5:31, 32

"For this cause shall a man leave his father and mother, and shall cleave to his wife and they shall be two in one flesh....

"This is a great sacrament; but I speak in Christ and in the Church."

14. Holy Orders

a. Luke 22:19

"And taking bread, He gave thanks and brake; and gave to them saying: This is my body, which is given for you. DO THIS FOR A COMMEMORATION OF ME."
(See 1 Corinthians 11:24)

b. John 20:21-23

"He said therefore to them again: Peace be to you. AS THE FATHER HATH SENT ME I ALSO SEND YOU.

". . . Receive ye the Holy Ghost. Whose sins you shall forgive, they are forgiven them; whose sins you shall retain they are retained."

c. Acts 6:5, 6

"And they (the disciples) chose Stephen . . . and Philip . . . and Nicholas. . . . These they set before the Apostles: and THEY PRAYING IMPOSED HANDS UPON THEM."

Acts 13:3

"Then they, fasting and praying and imposing their hands upon them [Paul and Barnabas], sent them away."

Acts 14:22

"And when they (Paul and Barnabas) had ordained to them priests in every church . . . they commended them to the Lord. . . ."
St. Paul's Precepts to Timothy:

d. I Timothy 4:14

"Neglect not the grace that is in thee, which was given thee by prophecy, WITH IMPOSITION OF THE HANDS. . . ."

I Timothy 5:22

"Impose not hands lightly upon any man. . . . "

e. 2 Timothy 1:6

"For which cause I (Paul) admonish thee, that thou [Timothy] STIR UP THE GRACE OF GOD WHICH IS IN THEE BY THE IMPOSITION OF MY HANDS."

f. Titus 1:5

"For this cause I (Paul) left thee (Titus) in Crete, that thou shouldst set in order the things that are wanting, and shouldst ordain priests in every city, as I also appointed thee."

www.ingramcontent.com/pod-product-compliance
Lightning Source LLC
LaVergne TN
LVHW051503080426
835509LV00017B/1896